Education in Western Culture

THE PROFESSIONAL EDUCATION FOR TEACHERS SERIES

Under the Editorship of PAUL WOODRING

Editor of the Educational Supplement of the Saturday Review,
and Distinguished Service Professor at Western Washington State College

PUBLISHED TITLES

Introduction to American Education, Paul Woodring

Education and Democratic Ideals, Gordon C. Lee

Education in Western Culture, Robert Ulich

American Secondary Schools, Mauritz Johnson, Jr.

Volumes on the following topics are in preparation: Elementary Education, Innovations in Education, Human Growth and Development, Learning in the Schools, Measurement and Evaluation, Social Psychology in Education.

Education in

Western Culture

ROBERT ULICH

Professor Emeritus, Harvard University

Harcourt, Brace & World, Inc.

New York · Chicago · San Francisco · Atlanta

12704

LA 11. U38

Editor's Foreword

When European culture was transplanted to the New World the colonists brought with them an ancient educational tradition. It had flourished in Athens, survived the fall of Rome, adapted itself to Christianity during the Middle Ages, and had taken new form in the grammar schools and universities of Elizabethan England. In America it has been modified repeatedly to meet the challenges of new frontiers and the changing social patterns of the eighteenth, nineteenth, and twentieth centuries. But much of the ancient tradition has survived through all the changes of two and a half millennia, and it continues to bring vitality to Western culture.

Without a knowledge of this long history a teacher cannot fully comprehend either his culture or his professional task. Though much of the needed understanding comes as a byproduct of a liberal education, a student preparing himself to become a teacher needs a single volume that brings the tradition more sharply into focus. The present volume, which is designed to meet this need, may be used in any of a variety of ways, depending on the organization of courses in the professional sequence. It may be used in conjunction with the first two volumes of the series in a course that offers a historical and philosophical introduction to education, or it may be used as the basic text in a short course in the history of education to be rounded out with a wealth of supplementary readings.

An author who is to interpret the educational traditions of an entire culture in a small volume must be a scholar of exceptional breadth, with a command of languages other than his own. In addition to being an educator, he must be both a historian and a philosopher. Professor Ulich is such a scholar. Born in Bavaria, he received his Ph.D. from Leipzig and taught in Germany for many years before coming to America. During his thirty years as a professor at Harvard he has come to be known and respected by

American educators for his distinguished contributions to both the history and the philosophy of education. In this volume he offers beginning teachers his mature interpretation of the role of education in Western culture.

PAUL WOODRING

Contents

Education in Western Culture

Chapter One

The Role of Education
in Social History

Most people feel that a school is a simple, uncomplicated institution. They envision teachers as regularly, if not richly, paid for explaining to pupils a prescribed and well-scheduled number of subjects. This kind of teaching—so they think—does not require much preparation, for it is repeated year after year. All children have the gleam of youthfulness and hope in their eyes, and though they may sometimes be bored and naughty, they generally obey instructions. Of course, a mother is sometimes concerned with the moral and intellectual conduct of her offspring. She may be profoundly convinced that it is the fault of the teachers, but she is not a customer who can cancel an order.

All this is taking place in and around buildings that vary in nature from the old and famous, albeit disappearing, little red schoolhouse, to the hundred-room monster built thirty years ago, to the handsome new plant designed by outstanding architects.

Indeed, to the casual observer the school is a world of its own— criticized, of course, as every human enterprise should be from time to time, but nevertheless peaceful in comparison with the conflicts and competitions of public life.

This picture is not entirely false. In our schools, so we hope, the clash of parties should not be heard. Our young people should establish roots in their community and culture, and for this they need quiet and protection. They may have anxieties about examinations, grades, and teachers, and perhaps about their parents as well, but only a brute would willfully destroy the green pastures in which childhood should prepare itself for the tasks of adulthood.

Yet every school transmits the values of the older generation to the younger. Because people often disagree about what should be learned and valued, education is involved in the drama of human history, with all its achievements and with all its conflicts and failures.

Today more than ever before it is necessary that we understand the interplay between the individual schools, the large currents in educational thought and policy, and the often violent changes in human culture as a whole. Instead of indulging in nice sentiments drawn from romantic memories of our own childhood, we should remember how often the hatreds of wars and revolutions, of races and creeds have inundated the halls of learning and endangered the lives of teachers and children.

The importance of schools is increasing constantly all over the world. Never before were they so much the guardians, sometimes also the challengers, of cultural heritage; never before have they formed the life and character of youth and even of adults as much as in our time, when the influences of family, church, community, and apprenticeship are constantly decreasing. Furthermore, with the rapid formation and rise of new nations that plan to move in one or two generations from illiteracy to literacy and from primitive agriculture to industry, schools are no longer merely the transmitters of heritage. Rather, they are actors in revolutionary constellations.

EDUCATION AND THE ENVIRONMENT

Who determines what should be taught, and in what spirit, and within what form of organization?

We must raise this question as the first among several, because we cannot understand the history of education without achieving some clarity with regard to the forces that control a school system. The obvious answer is that the school is dependent upon its environment, but the environment is many things: parents, neighbors, customs and habits, ambitions, emotions, ideologies, and especially the political powers that dominate the community. Whereas in some societies the political order tends to be rigid, static, and largely based on heredity, in others it is fluid and mobile. But some vertical line, some notion of low and high, exists always and everywhere.

In periods we generally call feudal, the kings, nobles, priests, and officials, often in alliance, ruled the nation and its education. Landownership was almost indispensable, because it was the main source of income. Only the priests were sometimes, though not always, an exception. In the Middle Ages, for example, the Church was the biggest proprietor of the soil.

In more modern times the accent has shifted toward industry and capital, which may or may not remain within the same family, and toward large associations such as manufacturers, labor unions, professional groups, or "cliques," all controlled, we hope, by constitutional instruments of executive, legislative, and judicial authority. Such associations try to establish and maintain some balance of power between conflicting interests, but they are never entirely free from the class structure of their country. In most recent times new forms of political organization have emerged in the form of totalitarian governments which, if the regime of the original leader and his immediate successors survives long enough, tend to become composites of dictatorship, bureaucracy, military, and interrelated collectives of limited advisory power.

The weight of the dominating group, which often descends from a conquering and aggressive minority as, for example, the old-European nobility, may long outlast its creativeness, because forms of government, authority, social relations, economic influence, and moral and religious conventions have, once they become established, a high degree of tenacity. Even in mobile cultures there remain vestiges of the old in the form of prestige symbols such as titles, and particular manners of speech and standards of taste. The more the group in power feels threatened by opposition groups, the more it will try to win the cooperation of the educators and, through them, of the younger generation. Whereas democracies try to turn the counterplay of forces into an interplay, in nondemocratic societies the struggle over the schools may assume violent forms.

In such societies the program of studies is carefully supervised; obstinate instructors are dismissed; opposing or unwelcome pupils and their parents are accused of subversive ideas; and public opinion is mobilized by means of fear-awakening slogans. The moment the old regime has been overthrown the victors begin to use the same tactics. In modern times these tactics are implemented by the increasingly powerful communications media: books, the press, radio, and television. In totalitarian nations news from foreign countries is banned as much as possible. Over the whole earth there has been thrown a network of propaganda and counterpropaganda that often goes under the name of education.

More than ever before the majority of teachers can easily be subdued because their salaries are paid by public institutions. Even private organizations cannot long withstand pressure, because their

income can be cut off by indirect means. Furthermore, social upheavals are generally connected with economic distress. Even under
the present conditions of relative prosperity the funds available to
the great universities all over the world do not suffice to pay for
scientific research. Thus, what could be more obvious than the
dependence of education on social structure?

Indeed, Marx and his followers, in accordance with their materialistic interpretations of history, have developed a definite
scheme of educational philosophy. During the Middle Ages, they
assert, the schools were dominated by the feudal class, and when
the bourgeois class replaced the older order, it in turn impressed
its pattern of interests or ideology on the schools. Logically, the new
communist society, too, will have to impose its philosophy on the
population and its schools. By some miracle this development will
end the class struggle and the concomitant capitalistic wars, and
a truly international world order will emerge. What could be
clearer and more inevitable than this? Things are not so simple,
however. As a matter of fact, no greater hindrance to worldwide
cooperation exists today than Marxian communism. The textbooks
used in the schools of Soviet Russia are filled with distortions and
expressions of hatred of noncommunist societies.

Democratic historians also suffer from the deterministic, though
supposedly scientific, milieu theory that molded the Marxian concept of education. They fail to see that schools are not entirely
dependent upon their environment; schools also make and form
the environment. Just as teachers need the political community,
so the community needs teachers. The inner dynamics of education
can never be fully explained in terms of politics and economics.

True, in the Middle Ages the change from isolated monastic
schools to universities was made possible by the rise of urban
islands within an agrarian environment and by the change from a
clumsy barter system to monetary forms of exchange. Furthermore,
the universities enjoyed the protection of the Church and the
monarchies. Yet, during their rise the universities and even the
minor schools fought the intrusion of the great powers upon their
freedom. In many cases the princes and the Church had to give in
because they needed learned men for administration, for the professions, and for the cultural life of the society. Furthermore, the
great universities such as Paris, Bologna, Salerno, Oxford, and Cambridge reached far beyond the boundaries of their own countries.
They were international, and they used Latin, the universal lan-

guage. Paris, at the very height of its fame, harbored not even one great teacher of French origin; all the teachers came from other countries. Not before 1474, about a hundred years after Paris had lost its great prestige as the theological and philosophical center of Europe and had begun to meddle in the political affairs of France, could King Louis XI order that the rector (which then meant the rector of the student body) become a subject of the realm.

As we shall see, sociological categories, while they may be of great importance for the understanding of the history of education, do not give us the whole picture. If exaggerated, they may even give us a false one. The intellect has its own inner momentum. As in religion, so in learning, there have always been men who stand above their environment. The rise of science would not have been possible without the martyrdom of some teachers and scholars—a martyrdom caused by the prejudices of clerics and laymen. Even under the Nazis, a little Bavarian teachers' journal managed to oppose the Hitler regime until shortly before the Second World War. Then its editors were silenced.

To be sure, the majority of people do not like to suffer. It is the martyrs who restore and preserve the dignity of humanity. Ultimately the environment does not feed on itself or on all those who are anxious to adjust themselves to it. Rather, it is the individual human being who makes the environment.

EDUCATION AND THE NATION

Educational systems are part of the political and ideological framework of a nation. This was not always so—certainly not in the Middle Ages. Even absolutist governments like those of France and Austria left schooling largely to the Catholic orders, which, of course, cooperated with the regime but were under the command of Rome. Moreover, for several hundred years Christian missions have maintained systematic forms of schooling on all the continents of the world, and on the secular level the number of international contacts is constantly increasing. The United Nations, UNESCO, and similar organizations have educational agencies in many countries, and so has the United States Peace Corps. However, the fact remains that on the whole educational systems work under national rather than international auspices.

But what is a nation? Many thinkers have written on this subject. Reading their works leads us to the conclusion that many of the criteria that we would otherwise be quick to apply are inadequate. Surely a nation is a political unit with a common government and common boundaries, although in many parts of the world minorities would prefer a nation other than the one in which they live.

Common ethnic origin, contrary to what some people believe, is certainly not a valid criterion. If it were, most nations of today could not so call themselves. Nor do nations necessarily have a common language, as is demonstrated by countries such as Belgium, India, and even the United States. Not all the citizens of a nation hold the same opinion about certain national features. There are monarchists in France who hate the revolution of 1789; conservatives in Germany, Austria, and Italy who are anything but convinced republicans; and republicans as well as monarchists in Franco's Spain. Parties split over political creeds; conflicting religious denominations have divided whole nations; and the Civil War is still a matter of controversy in this country.

Ultimately, a nation is a faith. A superior loyalty above minor loyalties, a sense of identity despite differences, must keep the people together like a chain that holds firm though it contains links of different size and color. If this faith is gone then the nation is also gone, even though it continues to exist legally.

Hence, imbuing the young with a uniting faith and tradition and placing them within a meaningful continuum—in other words, rooting the national future in the national past—this is what a people asks its schools to do. The schools should tell the story of the great men, victors as well as martyrs, who have formed the state politically as well as culturally, of the great ideas the nation has contributed to civilization, of the battles it has fought for its survival and aggrandizement, and—last but not least—of the sufferings it has endured. For just as common enjoyments and satisfactions make a nation, so also do common sufferings. It is the same as with friendships and family bonds; hardships voluntarily borne together add to their depth and truth.

EDUCATION AND THE ETHICAL PROBLEM

In our discussion of the relation of schools to the environment and the nation there was implicit a third historical factor: the responsibility of education to the moral conscience of a society. Schools are agencies of evaluation and selection, not only in terms of admission and grading, but also because society expects them to instill in the minds of the young criteria or values by virtue of which they can decide which environmental influences to accept or reject. Education is partly a process of adjusting, for society does not want maladjusted adults. But education that is nothing more than a process of adjusting is education for slaves, because only a slave has to accept without the responsibility of choosing.

Of course, criteria for choosing between the desirable and the undesirable are not determined by educators in isolation from their cultural and political community. Many, perhaps the most cherished, values in a civilization are not even the result of a conscious choice between obvious alternatives. Rather, they seem to be given, or inherent in life, because as members of larger social units we all share culturally inherited elements which are implanted so early that we take them for granted unless they are shaken or threatened by social upheavals.

Inevitably the schools then become involved, for both the defenders and the critics of the old try to use the schools for the confirmation of their ideas. Moreover, many teachers come from universities, and it is in the universities that new opinions are most often created and discussed.

In every crisis of history schools have played an active role. At the end of antiquity the Christian catechetical schools were the centers of cultural transformation. At the time of the Reformation the universities were the institutions that prepared the Protestant teachers. Later, the rationalist-humanist movement was supported by at least some of the institutions of higher learning. Teachers and teacher unions participated in the German liberal revolutions of 1830 and 1848, and the Bolshevists of 1917 could not have defeated the old regime without the cooperation of thousands of graduates from the Russian universities. The teachers in newly created schools in Asia and Africa will decisively influence the future of those continents.

Today we are experiencing a time of transformation that in magnitude and depth is second to none of the earlier transitions. In many countries this transformation was, still is, and will be fraught with violent conflicts. We hope, however, that nations with a democratic and "open" tradition will transform those conflicts into a productive evolution—unless first we all become engulfed in a third world war.

The causes of our present crisis in values have so often been explained that we need only allude to them here. We have gone through two world wars and mass persecutions that would have been considered impossible at the beginning of this century, and we have experienced political, scientific, and technical changes that have paradoxically brought the parts of the earth closer together while moving them farther apart. The older religious, idealistic, and humanistic systems of thought have been subjected to radical criticism, and the self-image of man has changed under the impact of new scientific and psychological theories. Moreover, modern historical and anthropological research, itself partly overwhelmed and confused by the mass of new discoveries, has shattered many old beliefs—beliefs that were, perhaps, prejudices from the scientific point of view, but nevertheless personally and socially integrating forces. Our Western civilization, with all its rational and political achievements, is no longer universally regarded as the Holy Grail of human values and achievements. Many people now want something else.

Thus the teacher must look at human history as at a colorful succession of cultures in which different peoples have cherished different ideals, idols, symbols, and banners, have had different places of pilgrimage—from the Madonna of Guadalupe to the Lincoln Memorial in Washington, D.C.—have expressed themselves differently through their languages, their myths, and their art, have been either monogamous or polygamous, have had different rules of kinship, of sex life, of labor and social control, and have had diverging opinions on war and its techniques. Often it is impossible to say which choices have been better than the others.

There are also great variations in the range of persons different societies have considered worthy of friendship, sympathy, and equality. We speak of the natural rights of man—that is, the natural rights of all men—but we must remember that Aristotle, the author of the most influential work on moral philosophy, the *Nicomachean Ethics,* could regard slaves as subhuman, without the slightest pangs of conscience. Slaves were also an object of trade for rich English merchants and for gentlemen of the southern

United States. Hitler sent millions of innocent Jews into the gas chambers, and all Western as well as many Eastern nations are responsible for the cruelty of enforced mass migrations and mass transportations. Furthermore, although advanced civilizations exceed primitive ones in their wider range of knowledge and technology, and consequently also in the choice of means, too often they have used these advantages not for the good, but for the misery, of men.[1]

We still cherish such traditional value concepts as freedom, progress, human dignity, and justice before the law. Although for many these concepts have preserved their weight, they are now threatened by slogans with a ring of skepticism and uncertainty about them: anxiety instead of courage, loneliness instead of community, longing instead of fulfillment, conformity instead of originality, and bewilderment instead of order. We speak of "lost generations." However, schools cannot succeed unless there is hope, a sense of progress, and a clear picture of what the human person is and what it should be. Actually, the sense of purpose is more certain in our grade schools than in our liberal-arts colleges. For what purpose do the colleges liberate? Only within the realm of the advanced professional courses is there order.

The drama of man is not just a record of change and contradiction. It can also be pictured as a continuum. Vital cultures have always felt the need for ideals at which to aim. In spite of differences in the appearance and content of their aspirations, they do have loyalties, symbols of faith and belief, the desire for love and kinship, and they have expressed their emotions by dint of art. After the wave of relativism that swept over the comparative studies of man and history during the past decades, our anthropologists discovered substantial similarities and identities within the large variety of human cultures.[2]

Schools that fulfill their function open the minds of youth to the fact that every constructive period of history has been a period of change, even of crisis. At the same time they teach that change invites chaos unless the present is connected with the past and unless there are goals toward which to strive.

---

1. M. Ginsberg, *Essays in Sociology and Social Philosophy,* 2 vols., vol. 1: *On the Diversity of Morals,* London: Heinemann, 1956.
2. C. Kluckhohn, *Mirror for Man,* New York: Whittlesey House, 1949.

EDUCATION AND REASON

Every generation learns from the work of earlier generations, unconsciously in early youth, but more and more consciously as the
stages of education advance. In the curricula of our schools there
are represented the thoughts and deeds of the ancient Jews,
Greeks, Romans, and those who later equaled them in productivity. Often the older has been modified, even distorted, yet
somehow it has survived.

This process of accumulation and re-creation of knowledge is
made possible by an ultimately mysterious phenomenon, for which
we have various names such as intelligence, mind, and reason. Man
can be a learner and discoverer only because there flows through
him and his history a conceptual or rational power, which the
Greeks called the *logos*. It is more than just logic. It includes disciplined intuition and imagination, and it has a transcendent quality that leads the mind beyond the visible toward the invisible.
Religion becomes superstition without reason, and without reason
art becomes trifle.

Whenever schools neglect man's capacity for reasoning, in the
comprehensive sense of the term, they impoverish humanity. Learning in its deepest sense is more than just learning this and that.
It is learning how to learn, to enrich one's soul, to widen one's
horizon, to ask bold questions, and to bring obstinate areas of
existence under one's comprehension.

As even the early Greeks knew, in its purest and most self-devel-
oping form reason expresses itself in mathematics. On mathematics
is based the gigantic development of science, from the simplest
forms of measurement to Einstein's formula of the unity of the
universe, from the simplest tools of craftsmen to modern missiles.
Nevertheless, the more reason ventures from the quantitative and
verifiable into hypothesis, the more it exposes itself to the possibility of error. Yet there can be no truth unless we accept the risk
of error. Many of our most passionate intellectual pursuits will
never reveal *the* truth—hence the infinity of search together with
its finiteness. Hence, also, the exposure of schools to the vicissitudes
and fallacies of the human mind.

It was the certainty of being close to truth that gave some of
the great religious prophets as well as the martyrs of science the
courage to suffer persecution. Ecclesiastical and political powers

could put bold thinkers into prison, chase them from country to country and burn their books, and even expose simple teachers to starvation. But, after some time, people felt they had been deprived of their liberty for search, which in morally advanced civilizations is regarded as one of the natural rights of man. For without this right survival itself is at stake. Untruth is dangerous.

Unfortunately schools have not always been centers of enlightenment. In the fight against tyranny they have been sometimes at the front, but usually at the rear. Yet even during periods of shame they have been silent revolutionaries against oppressors. For, when forced to teach false doctrines in certain portions of the curriculum, they could not be prevented from teaching logical thinking in others. Sooner or later, the contrast was discovered.

This inner order in learning—not necessarily what one learns, but *that* one learns—has always made reactionary powers suspicious of the spread of schools for the few and privileged to schools for the population at large. From their own point of view the reactionaries were correct, because learning and thinking mean comparing and looking for causes and consequences. And the critical mind is more difficult to govern than the uncritical.

THE PROGRAM OF STUDIES

The substance and mirror of the work of schools are found in their programs of study, or their curricula. There one finds the subjects to be learned, and, if a school system is as it should be, these subjects are ordered according to their importance, and in sequences leading from the basic to the more demanding topics, following the mental maturity of the students.

Today we hear such phrases as "curriculum making" or "curriculum makers," as if curricula could be organized like a business enterprise or constructed like a machine. A historical study of curricula reveals that they have reflected not only changes in knowledge and preferences in subject matter, but, as we have already indicated, changes in cultures as a whole. For, directly or indirectly, adults transfer into the curricula of their schools the lessons they have learned from their own lives and struggles. Thus a curriculum is both a testimony of fact and a testimony of aspirations, an instrument of the immediate and a lever of hope.

From a good program of studies pupils should learn that every step forward in their intellectual development leads them deeper into a community of men that has its origin in the distant past and aims toward distant futures, that speaks different tongues yet only one language, that can tolerate contrasting opinions because it is united by the same spirit, and that symbolizes the kind of immortality in which mortals of all beliefs and disbeliefs, races and spaces, may consciously share: the immortality of the Spirit.

All we have said about the history of education can be confirmed by an analysis of the history of curricula. We see there the dependence of education on its environment, but also its independence, its role as a transmitter, a mediator, and a renewer of culture. In the curriculum we observe the role of education in the affirmation and rejection of values, its involvement in political and moral crises, its exposure to both dogmatism and relativism, and finally its ability to provide a rational and self-accumulative continuum within all the discontinuities of human history. Therefore, the following remarks on the nature of the curriculum are more or less complementary to statements already made.

In all developed programs of study we find the polarity of "immediacy" and "transcendence." Immediacy exists where and when the curriculum relates to the visible and practical concerns felt within a society. Transcendence exists when teaching reaches beyond the environment and deals with foreign cultures and products of imagination. An amazingly large part of programs of study in earlier times resulted from the belief of responsible men that their culture needed the enrichment from originally foreign ideas perhaps even more than from its own resources, or that it needed the transference of the distant into the present.

As a matter of fact, all those immensely productive periods that we call classical came about when a nation had productively assimilated the universally great values it had discovered in other cultures. Such was the genesis of the Italian Renaissance, the Elizabethan Age, French classicism, and German idealism.

The most gigantic event of transcendence and assimilation was the acceptance of an originally oriental religion, Christianity, by the Occident. The intellectual and spiritual tradition of Greece and Rome withstood the impact to such a degree that historians argue over which molded Christian doctrine more decisively: the Old and New Testaments, or Greco-Roman philosophy. Thomas Aquinas, the canonical philosopher of the Catholic Church, called

Aristotle "the teacher." Nevertheless, Christianity defeated pagan polytheism and undermined the political structure of the Roman empire.

In contrast to the resistance of older civilizations, the Teutonic cultures were almost completely destroyed, though their mystical depths might have been capable of further development. The rupture would have been complete if the Christian forms of worship had not adapted themselves to older traditions. However, of this process of assimilation most of us are no longer aware.

There is still another example of the influence of distant values on our programs of study. One would suppose that the dominating class in a particular society would always insist that its ideas of government and social order be the central topics within the curriculum. However, during the whole Middle Ages Latin authors, and, from the Renaissance on, Latin and Greek authors provided by far the largest, if not the exclusive, bulk of reading. In the classical schools of Europe this tradition is still upheld.

Of course there were reasons for that tradition in earlier times. It was not altogether reverential idealism. The Middle Ages, partly even the Renaissance, would have been poor without the literature of antiquity and the church fathers, who were considered a part of it. This literature contained not only sacred knowledge but also the sciences, including the medicine of Hippocrates and Galen, the architecture of Vitruvius, and useful advice on agriculture and horticulture. The medieval schoolmen modestly considered everything they wrote a commentary on ancient writers.

This changed with the development of humanistic scholarship and the rise of science after the sixteenth and seventeenth centuries. Yet, if anything the curriculum of the secondary schools became still more oriented toward the classical languages, and the moderate protests of John Locke, Benjamin Franklin, and the German philanthropists under the leadership of Johann Bernhard Basedow did not change the situation. Even Herbert Spencer, who in 1861 in his book *Education: Intellectual, Moral, Physical* inveighed against the classicism of such aristocratic English Public Schools as Eton, Winchester, and Harrow, had little influence in his country. Only the teachers of the United States followed his suggestions for a more realistic curriculum.

Of course, one could here apply the doctrine of Marxian dialectical materialism, and the communist educators did not miss that

16

opportunity. They maintained that the insistence on the classical languages was a means of keeping the populace away from the schools and the professions of the privileged, of keeping privileged youth within strict discipline and a static state of mind, and of keeping both the privileged and the many from asking inconvenient questions about God, government, social justice, the nature of man, and the nature of nature. But, to choose only two examples, whoever reads the letters of Thomas Jefferson, with their many allusions to the classics, or the writings of Wilhelm von Humboldt, the reformer of the German *Gymnasium* and the founder of the University of Berlin and who left the Prussian government when it turned reactionary after the victory of Napoleon, whoever reads these writings must admit that they were not written by men of narrow minds. Rather, they were written by men who thought that the present would be richer, the future more promising, the world more united, and the continuum of progress better preserved if the leaders of nations were to learn about the wisdom, the beauty, but also the failures, of the mother nations of Western culture. They might thus be able to look with a sense of proportion at the problems of their time. This is the very requisite of productive realism.

Humboldtian classicism no longer gives us the answers we need in our world of science, democracy, and communism. Even in Humboldt's time it did so only for a few. Nevertheless, the question arises as to how long Western culture can survive if we no longer know about its roots, especially since Christianity too goes through a process of erosion.

It is only recently that the curricula of all schools—from the grades to the universities—have concentrated on the present. Fundamentally this change reflects the rapid accumulation of knowledge in our modern culture. It is no longer necessary to borrow from other sources. Commerce, trade, and agriculture at the time of Jefferson were more suggestive of the Middle Ages than of our own time. No one could have foreseen the impressions that the catapulting discoveries of science, communication, transportation, and global contacts would make on young minds.

Yet our culture is rich not only because there is so much around, but also because there was so much before and there will be so much ahead. If we want to understand a person and judge his future, we have to ask not merely what he is, but also how he has become what he is. Similarly, in order to have a program of studies that can serve as a design for the immense responsibilities of modern life, we have to add the vertical dimension of history to the horizontal dimension of the present.

Suggestions for Class Discussion and Further Investigation

1. Would it be possible to maintain a civilized society without formal education? Consider the examples of several non-Western civilizations before you draw a conclusion.
2. Is universal education essential to civilization?
3. Has the necessity for schools—as contrasted with the necessity for other institutions—increased or decreased in Western civilization over the past five or six centuries? Why?
4. Over the centuries has education been considered primarily a responsibility of national governments? What are the alternatives?
5. In what way has the growth of nationalism influenced the nature of formal education?
6. In a pluralistic nation who should decide which of the many values held by the older generations are to be transmitted to the young?
7. Consider the statement in the text, "In every crisis of history schools have played an active role." What crises does the world face today? What part are the schools playing in each?
8. If an effective world government were to be established, what changes in education might be expected in the United States? In other nations of the world?

Chapter Two

The Foundations

As we have already indicated, without some knowledge of the foundations one cannot understand the education of Western nations. For these foundations are not like a cellar to which we rarely go down; we still live in and with them more intimately than most of us realize.

THE GREEKS: EDUCATION FOR REASON

The Background. Western literature abounds with different and sometimes contradictory characterizations of the ancient Greeks, those amazing people who not only gave the European continent its name, from Greek mythology, but also gave it a good part of its culture. So abundant were their achievements as builders of states, law-givers, colonizers of the Mediterranean coasts, heroic fighters for freedom, thinkers, scientists, poets, sculptors, and architects that every period and every writer concerned with the interpretation and assimilation of Greek culture can select and evaluate according to its or his own bent. The Greeks meant something different to the Romans, the church fathers and the medieval schoolmen, the Renaissance Humanists, the leaders of the Reformation and Counter Reformation, the statesmen and orators of the American and French revolutions, the rationalists of the eighteenth century, and the idealists and romanticists of the nineteenth century.

Even if we try to limit our view to the achievements of the Greeks in the field of education proper, we can hardly arrive at complete objectivity. Education was for them a part of statecraft [1] and consequently so deeply woven into the fabric of their living that any attempt to abstract it as a special activity from the totality of their culture creates a distortion.

---

1. Aristotle, *Politics,* tr. by H. Rackham (Loeb Classical Library, 1932), Cambridge, Mass.: Harvard Univ. Press, Bk. VIII.

One best understands the Greeks and their unique influence on posterity if one realizes that theirs was a genius of observation, inquiry, and logical discrimination, combined with a genius of verbal and esthetic expression that lifted them high above their contemporary world. These qualities appear in whatever they did —their politics, their thinking, and their art. Because these qualities—though certainly fostered by collective interests—reside only in individuals, the Greeks represent the spirit of personality with all its magnificence and freedom, but also with all its vices. During the first half of the fifth century B.C. this spirit inspired them to repel the onslaught of Persian imperialism, but it also made possible an Alcibiades, one of the most unprincipled and eccentric individuals in history. To be sure, in their attempts at federalism the Greeks showed remarkable political wisdom, but their alliances never lasted more than a few years.

More perceptively than any other people, the Greeks asked within a relatively brief period all the basic questions with which the thought and education of cultured nations will be forever concerned. "The unexamined life," Socrates says in the *Apology*,[2] is not worth living."

We now know that the Greeks were not always original. They were indebted to the oriental wisdom of India, Babylon, and Egypt. Only a blind admirer would contend that they always gave the right answers. Some of their answers, like Plato's unnatural suggestions in the *Republic* concerning the life of the guardians of the state, were utopian and, if put into practice, would have been dangerous. We today have not found the right answers either. It may well be that profound questions guide humanity more effectively on the way toward productive and progressive thinking than do onesided answers.

Here are some of the many questions the Greeks asked: What is the human person? What is his relationship to himself, to destiny, and to the whole universe of mind and matter? What is the relation between the state, education, and the individual, and what should be the aim of education? How can the emotions and passions be molded into an all-round and balanced personality? What is the nature of authority—political, theoretical, and ethical? Can humans

---

2. Plato, *Apology*, in *Works*, tr. by H. N. Fowler (Loeb Classical Library, 1914), Cambridge, Mass.: Harvard Univ. Press, 38A.

ever have a just state? How should it be structured, and who should
lead it? What is truth, and by what methods can we attain it? Is it
perhaps a mere illusion? What is the soul, and what is its function?
What is the relation between intuition, metaphysics, religion, and
science? What do we mean by "God," or "the gods"? Should we
conceive of the world as monistic, dualistic, or pluralistic? Is it
endowed with purpose (teleological), or is it a mechanically working, causal nexus which we misinterpret if we endow it with such
human concepts as plan and goal?

Is thought the reflection of a transcendental and eternal realm
of ideas, or is it a merely subjective enterprise? Is there an absolute good, or is our conception of the "good life" relative to our
environment and our appetites? To what degree will reason, knowledge, and esthetic experience help us in the attainment of virtue?

If we survey Greek history from the early cosmological period of
philosophy in the seventh and sixth centuries B.C., when the
Greeks tried to comprehend the essence of the world by dint of
simple categories such as being versus flux and spirit versus matter,
to the late Hellenistic era with its bewildering variety of philosophical and religious schools, then we find that the fifth and fourth
centuries B.C. are those from which Western education has profited
most. It was the era of the Sophists, with Protagoras as their eminent
intellect, of Plato, who in his dialogues speaks through the mouth
of Socrates, and of Aristotle. When we listen to the first philosophical gropings of adolescents, we may hear interpretations of the
world similar to those of the early cosmologists; when we study
philosophy systematically, we do it in the shadow of Plato and Aristotle; and, when we call a person a stoic, an epicurean, an eclectic,
a skeptic, or an agnostic, we use the designations of the schools of
thought that flowered just before and after Christ.

If we now go back to the classical period of Greece, we find that
the Sophists, Plato, and Aristotle all agreed on a number of important points: The noblest office of the citizen should be the
service of the state. The aim of education should be the kind of
happiness that springs from an individual's ability to direct his
conduct according to rational principles discovered by the art of
dialectics. Finally, virtue, though essentially the product of right
reason, should be conceived of not merely as a theoretical but also
as a practical responsibility, not merely as a set of good intentions
but also as fitness to act accordingly.

Plato and Aristotle agreed that there are eternal verities, logical as well as spiritual, under the authority of which man should live. Plato, however, saw them embedded in a separate and transcendental realm of values, whereas Aristotle, more monistically and empirically minded than his teacher, was concerned with the problem of the interaction between universal values and the natural world. Ideas, according to Aristotle, should not be considered as entities existing apart from the individuals who use them. However, both believed that the human mind could understand itself best as the expression of a universal mind or *logos*. They therefore considered the contemplative life superior to the active.

It would be difficult to say which of the two, Plato or Aristotle, has had the more profound influence on Western thought. If one speaks of the development of reflective thought in general, their influences might be regarded as equal, though Plato was only indirectly known in the Middle Ages, whereas Aristotle was regarded as "the teacher" by the scholastics of the thirteenth to the fifteenth centuries. Plato, on the other hand, had his revival during the Renaissance and never lost ground. In the first paragraph of the essay, "Plato; or, The Philosopher," Emerson says:

> There was never such range of speculation. Out of Plato come all things that are still written and debated among men of thought.

If, on the other hand, one thinks specifically of education as learning, then Aristotle must be mentioned first. This is not merely because of the immensity of his observations, but also because of his classifications, which were responsible during more than two millennia for the design of the intellectual globe of the Western and the Arabic world. The main categories he used were: logic; first philosophy (metaphysics) as an inquiry into the nature of being and the relation between universals and particulars; and the study of reality, which is divided into physics, biology, ethics, psychology, and politics. From these categories the scholars of the greatest Hellenistic university, that of Alexandria, developed the "cycle of knowledge," which the encyclopedists of the early Middle Ages organized into the "seven liberal arts" (*septem artes liberales*), with grammar, logic, and rhetoric as the *trivium* or the "three ways," and music, arithmetic, geometry, and astronomy as the *quadrivium*, or the "four ways." The seven liberal arts still remain vaguely in the organization of our universities and colleges; even our high-school textbooks remind the historian of the Aristotelian scheme of knowledge.

The work of the Sophists has been much less esteemed by posterity than that of the two great idealists, Plato and Aristotle. Our word "sophistry" is witness to that fact. The Sophists were skeptical about the existence of eternal verities, and this lack of belief did not recommend their thought to later, Christian philosophers. Moreover, they doubted the capacity of the human mind to enter into the essence of reality, the Platonic Being of being. Their individualism, severing the human person from the divine order, inevitably tended toward relativism and offered no barrier against anarchical egotism. We associate with Protagoras the dictum, "Man is the measure of all things." The Sophists valued reason and intelligence less as means for disinterested contemplation than as means for proving oneself to be right even when one was wrong. Their emphasis on the arts of dialectic and rhetoric was not that of a philosopher but that of a trial lawyer.

Yet they were not without merit. They contributed to the clarification of nature and the validity of cognition. They were the creators of grammar and syntax, and as a result of their interest in the immediate they became, so to speak, the first specialists to divide the older, more mythical unity of thought into special disciplines of research. In this respect Aristotle was indebted to them. As a matter of fact, had not these "foreigners" who came to Athens to teach for money—a despicable thing to Plato—gained an increasing influence over the youth of the city, the Socratic–Platonic dialogues would have taken a different form. Perhaps they would not have been written at all. Certainly we would not have one of the most famous of them, the *Protagoras*. Both Socrates and Plato were motivated by the fear that the new trend toward sophism might contribute to the disintegration of the tradition that had made Athens the center of the Greek world.

Politically, Plato's endeavors were in vain. Athens was incorrigibly corrupt. Moreover, the small Greek city-states wasted their wealth and the flower of their youth in internecine warfare. Thus it happened that in 338 B.C., not more than a decade after Plato's death, the Greeks could be defeated by the Macedonian king Philip II and his son Alexander (who had been educated by Aristotle), and eventually, in 146 B.C., the Romans were able to incorporate Greece into their growing empire.

In contrast to the intellectual achievements of the Greeks, the institutional side of their educational system (if it was a system) as well as their social and political life belong to the past. Nevertheless, a discussion of some of their aspects may help us to understand the general significance of social factors in educational development.

The Greeks, and Athenians in particular, have often been praised for their "democratic" life; they often spoke about it themselves. In the same vein, however, we might praise early industrial England as democratic because it had a legal system, the Magna Carta, and a parliament, and because it allowed for the participation of a wider group of citizens in the affairs of the country than did the absolutist monarchies of Europe. Athens had the laws of Solon, and Sparta had those of Lycurgus; and both allowed many more men in the offices of the state than did the contemporary absolutist monarchies of Asia. Nor was it considered in Greece an offense of sacred tabus to dispute the nature and conduct of gods and of men. There were exceptions, of course: Socrates was condemned and executed for just such questionings.

Actually, the political and social life of all Greek city-states was up to the fifth century B.C.—in Sparta up to the fourth century B.C.—dominated by a hereditary elite that stemmed from conquering and land-owning warriors as we find them in Homer. The exclusive education of these *aristoi* (Greek, *aristos:* best) consisted of learning the use of arms, practicing gymnastics combined with ritual dance, and rehearsing the cult of gods and ancestors. Poets were venerated as the interpreters of the great deeds of the race and of the sacred myths, which described not only the battles between men and men, but also the eternal battle between men and fate. There was no sentimentality about these battles; destiny was as cruel as war. Destiny irrationally not only made the innocent guilty, but also punished them with merciless rationality. Tragedy in its purest form reveals itself in the *Orestea* by Aeschylus.

Even in the post-Homeric period when a new and more urbane social order emerged with the rise of the city-states, the old standards remained, just as feudal standards remained in post-feudal Europe and still exist there as tokens of prestige. Social rank was determined by a person's place in the military organization. Only those who could fight on horseback or as infantry soldiers in heavy armor (the hoplites) could be elected to higher administrative and ritual offices. Those who worked with their hands—the craftsmen and especially the laborers, not to speak of the many slaves [3]—were excluded. Engagement in trade was looked down upon, except indirectly through capital investment. In *The Laws* the archconservative Plato wanted even agriculture to be relegated to the slaves, whereas Aristotle, who otherwise shared Plato's opinions about prestige, had a higher opinion of the farmer's work.

However, the standards must have been relaxed during the period between the victory of the Greeks over the Persians in 479 B.C. and the beginning of the Peloponnesian War (431 B.C.). The poor plebeian Socrates, the son of a midwife, could serve as a hoplite. We are almost inclined to believe Pericles when, in his famous funeral oration, he praised Athens as the ideal democracy. But, as we gather from the *Apology*, Socrates never held public office; his reputation, good in the eyes of some and bad in the eyes of others, came from his role as an "examiner of men."

> . . . The young men who have the most leisure, the sons of the richest men, accompany me of their own accord, find pleasure in hearing people being examined, and often imitate me themselves, and then they undertake to examine others; and then, I fancy, they find a great plenty of people who think they know something, but know little or nothing. As a result, therefore, those who are examined by them are angry with me, instead of being angry with themselves, and say that "Socrates is a most abominable person and is corrupting the youth." [4]

The deeper reasons for the exclusiveness of the privileged must be explained by the Greek concepts of *arete* (goodness) and *kalokagathia* (unity between beauty and virtue). Both were thought to be unachievable for men who have to struggle with the necessities of life.

> . . . A person living a life of manual toil or as a hired labourer cannot practise the pursuits in which goodness is exercised. [5]

---

3. There are a great many estimates of the number of slaves in ancient Greece. The opinion that the Greek economy, like that of the Southern United States before the Civil War, was based on slavery is exaggerated. In the fourth century B.C. Athens was the most advanced city in manufacture and trade, and therefore also in slave employment. But it did not reach one-half of the free population. The free population of Athens at the time of Pericles was about 100,000. A large number of foreigners, perhaps 45,000, lived and worked in Athens, but they enjoyed no citizen rights.
4. Plato, *Apology, op. cit.*, 23C.
5. Aristotle, *Politics, op. cit.*, Bk. III, iii, 3, 1278A.

Goodness is here the generic term for the noble qualities as they appear in a person who has a liberal education and is generous, strong in body, and appealing in appearance. The person who could not reach these standards was despised as a *banausos*. The word "banausic" was used in the same sense in England up to the eighteenth century, and among German intellectuals and artists *ein Banause* is still the synonym for a narrow-minded Philistine.

Education. Just as in the schools of the European aristocracy in a later age, the young Greeks preparing for a noble life were in no way pampered. On the contrary, the warning of the poet Menander that the never-beaten man will not be educated was thoroughly heeded.

Except in the military monarchy of Sparta, where boys were taken over by the state at the age of seven, the elementary education of the young Greek was private and divided between the family and schoolmasters, who were mostly of low prestige. For adolescents beyond the age of fourteen there existed a secondary stage that provided a form of general education with the study of the poets and classical writers as its main subjects. After graduation the young citizen of the propertied classes and of honorable descent entered, generally at the age of sixteen, the *ephebia,* which lasted two years in the Periclean age but was later reduced to one year. The *epheboi* were given patrol duties along the frontiers and other missions in which they could prove themselves as future leaders. They lived in special houses connected with fields for sport and military exercises. Apparently they were organized in fraternities, and long-life friendships were often established among the members. The aim was to make brave soldiers, good administrators, and preservers of the greatness of Greek culture. For their intellectual enrichment the young men could choose a number of subjects taught by paid instructors. Mathematics probably played a central role because from the time of Pythagoras the Greeks had esteemed it as the purest of all the sciences; for Plato it was the prerequisite to all higher learning.

After leaving the *ephebia* the ambitious and promising young men went into the schools of the philosophers—not schools in the modern sense, but free gatherings of pupils around a famous teacher. Besides philosophy and grammar (a combination of philology and analysis of language according to the Sophistic tradition), rhetoric became increasingly important, though it had been suspect to Plato and Aristotle as intellectually dishonest—and rightly so.

In the Hellenistic period, dating from the conquests of Alexander to the end of antiquity around the fourth century A.D., education became increasingly formalized and separated from the national and military traditions. As a consequence the *ephebia* merged more and more with the areas of higher studies, but instead of the old unity of knowledge, which was still maintained by Aristotle in spite of his talent for classification, specialization appeared. Medicine in particular became a systematic and professional enterprise of the first magnitude.

After 33 B.C. a group of medical works under the name of the *Hippocratic Collection* circulated at the University of Alexandria. The same university harbored a group of famous mathematicians, Euclid among them. Although some modern writers use the term "Alexandrian" in a disparaging sense, indicating by its use pedantry, formalism, and lack of originality, they should not forget that Alexandria was the gathering place of the greatest minds of the time. Although it did not produce a Plato or an Aristotle (what university has?), it was largely responsible for transmitting at least a part of the wisdom of antiquity to later generations. There was not only specialization at Alexandria; there was universality of outlook as well. The large expanse of the Roman Empire provided the political conditions within which Stoic philosophy could develop the idea of the unity of mankind over and above the division of races and ideas. From Epictetus we have the first vision of a universal and rational society of men,[6] and it was in the intellectual climate of Alexandria that the church fathers Clement and Origen developed a Greco-Christian philosophy of a depth and liberality far beyond later theological achievements.

While it is unlikely that many students of the old-European classical schools have heard the name of the Phrygian Epictetus, or even those of Clement and Origen, they have certainly heard the name of Epictetus' contemporary, Plutarch, for few men have played a greater role in the moralist tradition of the West. Without the pompous obscurations characteristic of writers of the later

---

6. Epictetus, *The Discourses*, tr. by W. A. Oldfather (Loeb Classical Library, 1926), Cambridge, Mass.: Harvard Univ. Press, Bk. I, xiii.

Hellenistic period, this eclectic of wide erudition and considerable
civil merit, honored by the great emperor Hadrian, chose to write
on almost all topics that appeal to man's sense of virtue and courage, and that appeal to his curiosity about the multitude of strange
things around him, from the fish in the water to the stars in the
sky. Indeed, for anyone who wants an accurate picture of the
knowledge of Greco-Roman society at the time of Jesus the works
of Plutarch are indispensable.

In his *Parallel Lives* he sets forth the actions and ideas of the
moral and intellectual heroes who were the pride and glory of
Greece and Rome. The masters of the schools in which the leaders of Europe were trained could find no better source of inspiration for their pupils than the stories of Theseus and Romulus,
Lycurgus and Numa Pompilius, Pericles and Alcibiades, Alexander
the Great and Julius Caesar.

Whereas the stories in *Parallel Lives* are biographical, Plutarch's
Moralia contain, besides pseudoscientific curiosities often repeated
by the writers of the Middle Ages, a great number of essays that
could have been written only at a time when the furies of war as
well as the passions of creative inquiry had given way to a gentle,
saturated, and somewhat resigned attitude of mind.

One of the essays in the *Moralia* is entitled "The Education of
Children." [7] Nature, reason, and habit, Plutarch says, must combine
if good character is to be produced. "For nature without learning
is a blind thing, and learning without nature is an imperfect thing,
and practice without both is an ineffective thing." As always when
a civilization that has sufficiently matured to grant respect to children, Plutarch recommends that "encouragement and reasoning"
rather than "blows or ill-treatment" should be used as the means
of education. Therefore "unreasonable tasks which the children
find themselves unable to perform" should be avoided. Childhood
is not merely a preparation for adulthood; it is a value in itself.

The subjects of learning recommended by Plutarch are in the
Aristotelian-Hellenic tradition: a rounded-out general education
with philosophy at the center—philosophy conceived of as a practical as well as a theoretical discipline. We are reminded of Boethius'
famous *De consolatione philosophiae* when Plutarch praises philos-

7. Plutarch, *Moralia*, tr. by F. C. Babbitt (Loeb Classical Library, 1927), Cambridge, Mass.: Harvard Univ. Press, Bk. I, 5–69.

ophy as the only remedy "for the illnesses and affections of the mind." Somewhat rhetorically, like all his contemporaries, Plutarch also speaks of "the gods." But although as a member of a noble family he fulfilled priestly functions—he may even have been initiated into the Dionysian mystery rites—there is no real religious feeling in his seemingly pious phrases. Man's inner comfort could no longer be sought from the Olympians.

At a time when Epictetus was speaking of mankind as a worldwide and self-respecting community, Plutarch carried with him the social prejudices of earlier periods. The prejudices were, however, mellowed. To be sure, human society was, for him, divided into the privileged and the unprivileged, but the unprivileged were nevertheless not mere humus. Slaves, who were already being used in the management of farms and commercial enterprises, could, if "sound in character, of Greek origin, and distinct of speech," become the companions of the young masters. Epictetus himself was a slave in his youth. Nevertheless, the moral ambiguity even in improved slave conditions appears in the following sentences:

> . . . We should, as a most sacred duty, accustom children to speak the truth. For lying is fit for slaves only, and deserves to be hated of all men, and even in decent slaves it is not to be condoned.

Concerning the education of the poor, Plutarch has this to say:

> My dearest wish would be that my scheme of education should be generally useful; but if some, being needy in their private circumstances, shall be unable to avail themselves of my directions, let them lay the blame therefore upon fortune. . . . Even the poor must endeavour, as well as they can, to provide the best education for their children, but, if that be impossible, then they must avail themselves of that which is within their means.

Let us be just. The opinions expressed in these sentences seem to us merciless, but they show a higher degree of social awareness than do many educational documents of Christian societies since then.

THE ROMANS: EDUCATION FOR ORDER

The Background. In contrast to divided Greece, Rome understood the power of unity. At the very beginning it was a small settlement of farmers and traders, situated in the swampy Campagna at the mouth of the Tiber. After the expulsion of the Etruscan kings,

around 500 B.C., Rome went through the usual class struggles between the hereditary aristocracy and the plebeians, and after severe
defeats the Romans succeeded in subduing the surrounding nations
by use of their superior military organization. The growing empire exploited its citizens ruthlessly in wars of conquest and thus
created that proletarian mass of homeless peasants and slum dwell-
ers who for centuries were the curse of Rome and the whole of
Italy. Finally, it organized around the Mediterranean a gigantic
commonwealth in which, during the centuries after Christ, every
inhabitant enjoyed the rights of citizenship, whether resident in
Greece, Africa, Asia, Spain, or Gaul.

Whereas Greeks, especially the Athenians and the Ionic Hellenes
of Asia Minor, had early contact with the richest civilizations of
antiquity and a script and language that made possible the communication of universal ideas, Rome began, so to speak, from
scratch. Studying and reading were held in low respect by this
practical people. *Docere non habet dignitatem;* that is, teaching
was below a man of status.

When in the second century conquest led to Greece and the Hellenistic countries, Rome was conquered by the culture of its former
enemies. Its own rural-puritanical tradition had been augustly expressed by the elder Cato, nicknamed "the Censor" for his fight
against luxury and his hatred of the first Greek philosophers who
entered Rome. So much was he venerated as a symbol of the old
Roman virtues that as late as the fourth century A.D. an unknown
author sought prestige by ascribing his own moral maxims to Cato.
Indeed, Cato's maxims were read in schools for many centuries, and
Benjamin Franklin published a translation by James Logan in 1735
with the title *Cato's Moral Distichs.*

Despite the moral strength of the elder Cato's philosophy, it soon
became too narrow for the growing empire. The great Scipio family, whose tomb can be seen in Rome, read Greek literature and
collected Greek books. Romans of influence founded libraries, and
Greek became the second language of the educated. After the middle of the second century B.C. no resistance to Greek culture was
offered, and the development of an authentic Roman culture was
arrested. Indeed, the Romans produced no original philosopher or
scientist. However momentous may have been the influence of
Latin poetry on posterity, it was even at its best a synthesis between
the Greek and Roman traditions. Even Vergil, who has been vener-

ated by posterity as the God-inspired prophet of Christ and the
Christian era, borrowed from the Greeks.

Thus, Cato and his followers had the same experience as had
Socrates and Plato when they tried to keep the Sophists away from
Athens: they were defeated. Even the major Roman deities Jupiter,
Juno, and Venus wore the mantles of Zeus, Hera, and Aphrodite.
Only Cato's emphasis on the family as the foundation of the state
survived rapid Hellenization, until that institution, too, was at last
undermined by luxury, wealth, and the mass immigration of for-
eigners and slaves.

Education. Just as the Hellenic states gradually abolished the military character of the *ephebia,* so also the Romans allowed the early
military character of their education to disappear. Many of the
privileged withdrew from service; the old military gymnastics became a sport. At the turn of the first century B.C., when the
Numidians and some Germanic or Celtic tribes defeated the Roman armies, the General Gaius Marius complained that the characteristic of a Roman noble was that he was a man of ancient
lineage with many ancestral portraits but no campaigns.[8] For the
older Romans the *vir bonus* (good man) or the *vir constans et
fortis* (steadfast and brave man) had been the pattern of emula-
tion; now it was the "orator." Cicero had written three treatises
on the art of speaking,[9] extolling its tradition and responsibility,
but about a hundred and thirty years later the statesman and historian Tacitus found much reason to deplore its corruption. That
corruption was, according to him, caused by "the laziness of our
young men, the carelessness of parents, the ignorance of teachers,
and the decay of the old-fashioned virtue." [10] The concentration
of power in the hands of a single ruler—Tacitus said, looking nos-
talgically back at the old republic—had produced a dishonest and
artificial mode of life and eloquence. True eloquence died with
Cicero. Men of integrity renounced the forum altogether.

Although he does not mention the name, Tacitus praises the

---

8. Sallust, *The War with Jugurtha,* tr. by J. C. Rolfe (Loeb Classical Library,
    1955), Cambridge, Mass.: Harvard Univ. Press, ch. lxxxv, 10, p. 33.
9. Cicero, *Brutus, Orator,* and *De optimo genere oratorum,* in vol. 2 of *Rhe-
    torica,* ed. by A. S. Wilkins, Oxford: Oxford Univ. Press, 1935.
10. Tacitus, *A Dialogue on Oratory,* in *Dialogus de oratoribus, Agricola, Ger-
    mania,* tr. by W. Peterson (Loeb Classical Library, 1914), Cambridge, Mass.:
    Harvard Univ. Press, p. 89.

Spanish-born Quintilian, whose *Institutio oratoria (Institutes of Oratory)* contains the most thorough survey of Hellenistic-Roman education we possess. Nevertheless, the way from substantiality to formality was completed. Of course, according to Quintilian, the orator should have gone through the "cycle of knowledge" or the seven liberal arts which the Hellenistic culture considered essential to an all-round education. He should also be "a good man." One feels, however, the fallacy of the emphasis. Style comes first. Whereas the Stoic Seneca the Younger preferred death to servility under a tyrannical monarch, Quintilian was a sycophant. The impression of showmanship increases when we try to translate the orations and eulogies of the later Hellenic period into honest English.

The gigantic, polyglot, and polyethnic realm of the Caesars had to be administered by career officials who had received practical, juridical training outside the schools of the theoreticians and rhetoricians. However, the latter were still officially recognized. Together with the philosophers and *grammatici* they enjoyed certain privileges and received salaries. Only the despised elementary teachers had to sell, like shopkeepers, their rudimentary knowledge in private enterprise.

If, thus, most Roman education was influenced by the Hellenistic spirit, how could Roman civilization have become one of the foundations of Western culture?

There are several answers. One is that Latin, the Roman language, developed into the lingua franca of the whole Western part of the medieval world. What the Romans learned from the Greeks they translated into their mother tongue, which was to be used for more than fifteen hundred years in the universities and princely chancelleries and which was to be regarded as the sacred language of the Catholic Church.

Unfortunately, the Romans did not share the Greek interest in science, which is the reason for the poverty of medieval scientific knowledge. Nevertheless, the Romans were builders in the grand manner. For two thousand years the travelers of Asia, Africa, and Europe have continued to use the roads constructed by the Romans. Moreover, the Romans established an admirable international postal service. We still admire their architecture, less lofty and delicate than that of the Greeks, but no less impressive, especially when we try to imagine the buildings in their original splendor of precious metals and travertine. At the time of Christ the city of Rome received many times as much water from its aqueducts as New York or London receive from their modern installations. Because of its ancient engineers Rome is still "the city of fountains."

These are only the external signs of the Roman sense of structure and order. The imperium, though first a work of conquest, became a masterwork of organization. It survived even its official demise, which occurred in 476 A.D. When, in 800, Charles the Great (Charlemagne) accepted the crown from Pope Leo III and thus revived the office of Emperor of the West, he hoped to revive at the same time the greatest tradition known to the people of the early Middle Ages. However unfortunate the political history of the Holy Roman Empire of the German Nation may have been, it nevertheless inspired Christians up to the seventeenth century to believe that Europe might be more than a mere conglomerate of fighting nations. Indeed, the fact that all the jealousy of kings could not kill the conception of "Europe" as a supernational unity—just as "Hellas" survived the wars of the Greek city-states—is largely due to the memory of the reign of the Roman Augusti over the multitude of peoples. For at no other time in history has the human race enjoyed a peace so enduring as the *Pax Romana* under great emperors disciplined in Stoic philosophy, and even under weak and cruel tyrants. Moreover, at a time when Greek thought was near exhaustion, the Romans provided, through their juridical language and canons, the basis for a systematic science of law. This system was not merely a matter of legality, for it helped form the conceptions of right and wrong that were recognized by civilized nations.

All this could not have been achieved by mere juridical and administrative dexterity. One can, without a sense of justice, manipulate the paragraphs of the law and even pervert them, but only if inspired by the will to justice can one make laws that will influence the world. Behind the *Pax Romana* and its *corpus juris* stood the Ciceronian concept of *humanitas,* which embodied the universal values by which mankind can lift itself over and above the animal state to the state of dignity and freedom.

In the third book of Cicero's dialogue *De republica*—written even before Epictetus had expressed the Stoic conception of the unity of mankind—one of the interlocutors says:

> True law is right reason in agreement with nature; it is of universal application, unchanging and everlasting; it summons to duty by its commands, and averts from wrongdoing by its prohibitions. . . . It is

a sin to try to alter this law, nor is it allowable to attempt to repeal any part of it and it is impossible to abolish it entirely. We cannot be freed from its obligations by senate or people, and we need not look outside ourselves for an expounder or interpreter of it. And there will not be different laws at Rome and at Athens, or different laws now and in the future, but one eternal and unchangeable law will be valid for all nations and all times, and there will be one master and ruler, that is, God, over us all, for he is the author of this law, its promulgator, and its enforcing judge. Whoever is disobedient is fleeing from himself and denying his human nature, and by reason of this very fact he will suffer the worst penalties, even if he escapes what is commonly considered punishment.[11]

No wonder the Christian fathers extolled Cicero as one of the harbingers of the Christian gospel, for in the *De republica* and in his other legal treatises this great Roman proclaimed the supremacy of the moral conscience over the laws of earthly government. A hierarchy was established which, despite all our sins against it, has provided the fundamental principle of truly human culture.

THE JEWS: EDUCATION FOR THE COVENANT

In one respect there is no difference between the ancient Jews and the ancient Greeks and Romans. All three believed they had been chosen by destiny for a particular mission. In their creative periods all three were race- and class-conscious, nationalistic, and insistent on pure blood. Apparently this was the condition of survival in early societies.

Today, however, none of the three cultures is praised for its exclusiveness. What we admire are their contributions to humanity. The Jews have been able to reach into the depths of the Western soul because of their passionate belief in and struggle with "the One God," to whom they felt related by dint of an eternal covenant.

This covenant was first interpreted to the Jews by Moses, who lived in the second millennium B.C. In spite of all the mist that surrounds his personality, he must be credited as one of the greatest lawgivers in history. Besides the Mosaic Covenant and the Ten Commandments, the Jews received through Moses a code of laws (Exod. 21–23) which, according to modern research, is a local adaptation of the civil laws of the Babylonians, the Assyrians, and the

---

11. Cicero, *De republica, De legibus,* tr. by C. W. Keyes (Loeb Classical Library, 1928), Cambridge, Mass.: Harvard Univ. Press, Bk. III, xxiii.

Hittites. According to Leviticus Moses also received from the Lord
the statutes and ordinances of holiness. "Ye shall be holy: for I
the Lord your God am holy." (Lev. 19:2) The statutes add to the
rather negative Ten Commandments the positive demands of
neighborly love (Lev. 19:18), reverence, justice, righteousness, and
mutual help, together with a host of ritual instructions and pro-
hibitions that could be followed only by a privileged group, with
"the priests, the sons of Aaron" (Lev. 21:1) at the top of the hierarchy. Despite existing social distinctions, Moses gave to his people
a strong and divinely enforced sense of community. Whereas the
Greeks did not hesitate to make slaves of other Greeks, none of
the children of Israel was to serve as a slave. (Lev. 25:39–46)

Among no other people did education permeate the daily life of
the common man so completely as it did among the Hebrews. In
Deuteronomy 6:4–7 we read:

> Hear, O Israel: The Lord our God is one Lord:
> And thou shalt love the Lord thy God with all thine heart, and with
> all thy soul, and with all thy might.
> And these words, which I command thee this day, shall be in thine
> heart:
> And thou shalt teach them diligently unto thy children, and shalt
> talk of them when thou sittest in thine house, and when thou walkest
> by the way, and when thou liest down, and when thou risest up.

The monotheistic concept of deity and of chosenness has had
decisive consequences for all Western civilization and its education.
This concept carries with it not only a high sense of mission, not
seldom perverted, but also a sense of rationality. For, once the
supernatural premises of monotheism have been accepted, there
follows the conception of an indivisible hierarchy which cannot
fail to influence the total mental attitude. The idea of a divine
center must reject any contradiction to its unity. That which does
not fit into the structure must be wrong, or, in theological terms,
heretical. As history has sadly shown, the danger of intolerance
looms large, but there also arises a sense of distinction. Thus, Jewish
monotheism could not tolerate the worship of idols that was cus-
tomary among the surrounding nations, or the augury and witch-
craft that the Greeks and Romans practiced abundantly. We read
in Leviticus 19:26, "neither shall ye use enchantment, nor observe
times." No doubt pagan polytheism possessed more beauty and
depth than our Western lack of mythical imagination permits us to

believe. It was nevertheless precariously pitted against the great cosmogonic and idealistic systems of the Greek genius, and it finally dissolved into a variety of mystical rituals. In contrast, Judaism and its derivative, Christianity, could absorb much of Greek philosophy without losing themselves. At the time of Christ the Jewish philosopher Philo of Alexandria, who greatly influenced later Christian thought, attempted to prove the affinity between Greek thought and the Hebraic tradition.[12] A hundred years later the Gospel According to St. John could dare unite the Divine Principle with the Greek *logos* by saying, "In the beginning was the Word."

The monotheistic religions, however, could not free themselves from the magical tendencies in man, and thus they ran into conflict with later scientific and empirical developments. We still suffer from this conflict. It is at the same time no mere conjecture to say that it was monotheism which made room for a unifying and scientific aspect of life. Only on its foundation could the ideas of Copernicus, Spinoza, Hegel, Darwin, and Einstein have arisen. There is nothing comparable to them in polytheistic cultures.

Out of Israel's theistic spirituality, enhanced by its political tragedy, the prophets of the first half of the millennium before Christ rose to a height of religious and aesthetic sublimation that places them at the apex of the world's literature.

Isaiah enjoined his people (Isa. 1:11, 18):

> To what purpose is the multitude of your sacrifices unto me? saith the Lord: I am full of the burnt-offerings of rams, and the fat of fed beasts; and I delight not in the blood of bullocks, or of lambs, or of the goats. . . .
> Come now, and let us reason together, saith the Lord. . . .

Finally from Isaiah's mouth there came the words that have been used as a motto by the United Nations (Isa. 2:4):

> And he shall judge among the nations, and shall rebuke many people: and they shall beat their swords into plowshares, and their spears into pruninghooks: nation shall not lift up sword against nation, neither shall they learn war any more.

Naturally, Mosaic monotheism profoundly affected the attitude of its believers toward the problems of man's existence and education. No one can definitely say to what degree the Greeks and

---

12. H. A. Wolfson, *Philo: Foundations of Religious Philosophy in Judaism, Christianity, and Islam,* Cambridge, Mass.: Harvard Univ. Press, 1947.

Romans felt inwardly protected by the worship of their major and minor gods and goddesses. It is certain that Homer, Aeschylus, and even Vergil imagined man as dependent on unpredictable, contradictory, and revengeful forces. Plato, despite all his conservatism, felt uncomfortable with the thought that Greek youth should be educated in the shadow of Homeric mythology; its gods soon became an occasion for laughter among the sophisticated. Even in earlier times the Greeks had been convinced that the gods, no less than mortals, stood under the sovereignty of a dark and inscrutable power, *moira*. A cruel determinism was behind the colorful picture of the Olympian deities.

In contrast, even in calamity the Jews and later the Christians felt the nearness of the God who had made his covenant with them. He was the protector even when he punished. Though stern, he could not be capricious as Zeus or Poseidon often were. There was always the *justitia dei,* threatening, but also understanding.

From the idea of the covenant there were bound to develop the concepts of sin and guilt which have played such an important role in the Western educational tradition. These concepts have sometimes had an unhealthful influence on the development of a balanced and self-relying character; they have been used by Christian educators to arouse fear rather than hope. Nevertheless, they have refined the Western conscience. Even many of those to whom these transcendental ideas mean little or nothing still adhere, consciously or unconsciously, to values about which the lawgiver Moses spoke to his people more than three millennia ago. Jesus, who criticized the Pharisees for their formalism, nevertheless claimed that he had come "to fulfill the law."

THE CHRISTIANS: EDUCATION FOR SAINTLINESS

The Background. It is one of the most amazing revolutions in human history that the legacy of a crucified Jewish prophet survived the competition of a large number of powerful religions that attracted the mystical mood of the Hellenistic world, religions such as the cults of Mithras, Isis, and the Eleusinian mysteries. It not only defeated its religious competitors but also conquered the empire of the Augusti and, subsequently, the whole Western world. Without Christianity this so-called Western world—a highly inadequate, yet indispensable term—would not have come into being. It was this common faith, constantly violated, misused, but nevertheless surviving, which built an arch of unity over the warring nations of Europe and those parts of the world to which, as a consequence of explorations, missions, and migrations, the Christian gospel was extended.

There must have been felt in this gospel a depth, an invitation, and a challenge more comprehensive than that of ancient polytheism and philosophy. Indeed, whatever the wealth of religious and intellectual symbols that Asia, Africa, and Greece had developed, none of them provided for the faithful the sense of security of which we have already spoken in relation to the Jewish religion. Christianity offered even a stronger affirmation of the covenant between God and man than did the Old Testament, for it declared that the Divine Principle itself had appeared in the flesh to lead mankind toward salvation. Both the abstractions of Platonism, which only the educated could understand, and the unfulfilled Jewish expectations of a messiah were now replaced by a belief in a new and final epoch.

As we see from the writings of the church fathers, once a person had made the leap from pagan myth and thought, or from Judaism, to Christian faith, he believed that he possessed an explanation of all the mysteries that troubled the Hellenic mind: death, judgment, resurrection, and immortality.

Christianity also offered the believer the solution of a metaphysical problem that had tortured the minds of the Greek tragic poets and the authors of the Book of Job and Ecclesiastes, that is, the problem of suffering. Why did the gods, or Jahweh, allow the just to suffer while the sinners enjoyed the fruits of their misdeeds? How could evil exist and often even overcome good?

Man, according to Christian and Jewish doctrine, had no right to judge divine dispensation on the grounds of his own limited experiences. Human life was but a brief and finite span in the infinity of being. That which appeared as suffering here was, so the Christian believed, to reveal itself as mere trial on the day of judgment. The Son of God himself had died on the cross. So far went the *imitatio Christi* that the early Church had to warn some of its followers not to expose themselves unnecessarily to the sacrifice of martyrdom. When the day of judgment came, God, who looked into the hearts of men, would know how to separate the just from the unjust. He would send the faithful to a heaven of bliss, and the unjust to eternal damnation. This day, so the early Christians were convinced, would come soon. Wrote Paul to the Romans (Rom. 8:18) "For I reckon that the sufferings of this present time are not worthy to be compared with the glory which shall be revealed in us."

The persecution of the Church by the state could, of course, have no other effect on Christianity but to reaffirm its conviction of the end of an era of vice and of the desperate struggle of a government to which the God-related conscience should not submit. This conscience expressed itself concretely in the refusal of the Christians to adore the image of the emperor, which for the Romans was the symbol of the sovereignty of the commonwealth.

In essence the Christian principle of ethical supremacy was in no way new; as we know, it had already been expressed by Cicero and Epictetus, and it will always prevail when and where the mind of man transcends regional boundaries and arrives at a deeper understanding of the role of the self within mankind and of mankind within the cosmos. In the form of the concept of "the natural rights of man," it has become the ethical foundation of secular democracy. Some tension will remain even under the best historical conditions, for all institutions are tempted to arrogate to themselves the right to direct the thinking of their members and the education of their youth because one cannot govern without some measure of persuasion. If persuasion does not work, one may use force. The fundamental difficulty lies in the fact that even nontotalitarian institutions may honestly believe that they possess the truth and the right to impose that truth on everybody.

Least of all have the Christian churches themselves been free from confusion. Mistaking the finite for the infinite, they have done immense harm not only to their real or supposed enemies (who often were more inspired than those who looted their cities in the name of the true God) but also to themselves. According to John (John 14:2) Jesus had said, "In my Father's house are many mansions." Neither John's liberality nor Paul's gospel of love, expressed in his Epistle to the Corinthians (I Cor. 13), suggested clemency to the Inquisition.

Nevertheless, because the expected day of judgment did not arrive, the Christian communities had to find ways of coexistence between their Hellenistic environment and their civil and educational policy. Even the intransigent needed commercial and cultural contacts and did not wish to educate their children in complete isolation.

Education. The early form of Christian education was that of catechization—i.e., the question-and-answer system that in various forms has survived changes of instruction from the time of Socrates to our own day. The purpose of Christian catechizing was to secure the convert's insight into the meaning of Christian saintliness and salvation. Moreover, somewhat in the manner of the Hellenistic mystery cults, the convert had to go through a prescribed course of rituals before he could be baptized and admitted to the most sacred symbol of man's community with Christ, the Eucharist.

The great masters in the art of catechizing were the church fathers Origen and Augustine. Of the teaching practice of both we have ample testimony. In his *Panegyricus in Origenem*,[13] Origen's disciple Gregory Thaumaturgus revealed that the church father insisted on a broad knowledge of Greek science, literature, and philosophy before prospective leaders of the Church could be led into the final synthesis of all knowledge, the Christian faith. Of Augustine we have, among other writings with a similar purpose, his treatise *On the First Catechetical Instruction* (*De catechisandis rudibus*).[14]

Whereas Origen's approach is more intellectual, that of Augustine is, in accordance with his personal temperament, more emotional. He insists on three stages of instructional development: listening must lead to faith, faith to hope, and hope to love, as manifested by God himself in the Old Testament, but especially in the sacrifice of his Son.

For the purpose of initiating the beginner into God's revelation, Augustine includes also a more systematic and historical part. The convert must become acquainted with the covenant, the rise of the Christian communities, the appearance of the apostles and the martyrs, the mystery of resurrection, and the final victory of the

13. Gregory Thaumaturgus, *Address to Origen,* ed. by W. C. Metcalfe, New York: Macmillan, 1920.
14. Augustine, *On the First Catechetical Instruction,* tr. by J. P. Christopher, in *Ancient Christian Writers: The Works of the Fathers in Translation,* ed. by J. Quasten and J. C. Plumpe, Westminster, Md.: Newman Press, 1946.

Holy Trinity over the powers of evil. But all learning, Augustine
says, will be of no avail unless the disciple applies it in his daily
life. He should avoid all sin, not because of fear of punishment,
but because sin separates man from divine love and peace. Sin is
alienation.

At the time of Augustine the older forms of initiation into the
communio sanctorum had already relaxed. When infant baptism
more and more replaced the baptism of adults, the more severe
forms of conversion gave way to the cooperation of the family, the
Church, and the Hellenistic schools, which harbored an increasing
number of Christian teachers.

Of course, this process of *rapprochement* did not occur without
strife. Some of the church fathers refused any compromise with the
pagan tradition. According to the Syrian Tatian, of the second century, and a number of Africans, such compromise was more or less
the work of the devil. The little that was good in it had been stolen
from the Jews. Even more enlightened writers, such as Justin
Martyr, who suffered martyrdom under the reign of Marcus Aurelius, tried to explain the monotheistic trend in pagan philosophy
by asserting that the Greeks had borrowed the higher truth from
Moses, about whom they had heard in Egypt.[15]

Fortunately for the future of Western civilization, the moderate
wing, impressively represented especially by Clement of Alexandria
and his disciple Origen, succeeded in reconciling the Greek with
the Christian tradition, though, of course, not without strong res-
ervations about the hedonistic aspect of pagan literature. Even the
fanatical Tertullian, however, had to admit that Christians needed
"the knowledge of literature" for their professional life, as well as
for "efficiency in action."[16]

It is because of the resulting syncretism that, after the collapse
of the Roman empire, a sufficient knowledge of ancient philosophy
was saved to provide both our secular society and Christian theology with the degree of rationality without which a culture cannot persist.

15. Justin Martyr, *Hortatory Address to the Greeks,* in *The Ante-Nicene Fathers,*
    ed. by A. W. Roberts and J. Donaldson, Grand Rapids, Mich.: Eerdmans,
    1887, vol. 1, ch. xx, p. 281.
16. Tertullian, *De idolatria,* in *Patrologiae latinae,* ed. by J. P. Migne, Paris
    1844–55, Bk. I, ch. x, p. 751.

Suggestions for Class Discussion and Further Investigation

1. What is meant by the statement, "Education was for them [the Greeks] a part of statecraft"?
2. Both Plato and Aristotle have had a profound influence on education in the Western world for the past two millennia. How has the influence of Aristotle differed from that of Plato?
3. To what extent did the Romans borrow their educational traditions from the Greeks?
4. What were some of the most significant differences between Greek and Roman education? How do you account for these differences?
5. What were the essential differences between the educational views and practices of the early Christians and those of the Jews of the same period?
6. Trace the history of the use of catechisms from the earliest times to the present day.
7. What educational principles or assumptions underlie the use of catechisms? Is the use of a catechism consistent with the goals of liberal education? Why are catechisms rarely used in higher education?
8. From your knowledge of the decline and fall of the Roman Empire, do you conclude that the deterioration of education precedes, is concurrent with, or follows the decline of a civilization? What does Gibbon have to say about this?

Chapter Three

The Middle Ages:
Education for Hierarchy

THE BACKGROUND

One can best understand the Middle Ages by viewing it as a period whose mission was to bring order out of the chaos of forces that had concentrated on Western civilization since the breakdown of the Roman Empire. As with all great historical periods, there is no possibility of ascertaining the beginning or the end of the Middle Ages. Some historians choose the year 375 A.D., because of the beginning of the migration of the Teutonic tribes. But such migrations had threatened the boundaries of Rome since the invasions of the Cimbri and Teutones during the decade before 100 B.C. Others emphasize the year 476, when the last Roman emperor of the West, Romulus Augustulus, was deposed by the Germanic chieftain Odoacer, who was recognized by the Eastern emperor Zeno as *patricius* of Rome and prefect of Italy. But for a hundred years and more the West Roman emperors had already depended on the support of unreliable generals and, moreover, on the recognition of the East Roman empire, which for more than a century had been separated from the West without sharing in the latter's disintegration.

Culturally and educationally, the most consequential event was the official recognition of Christianity as the state religion by the East Roman emperor Constantine the Great, together with the convocation of the first ecumenical council of the Church at Nicaea in 325, which ended with the declaration of the *Symbolum Nicaenum*. For at this period paganism had been definitely defeated, and the Athanasian dogma of the Trinity established against heretics among the Christians themselves. Only by means of such a firm and binding creed could the Church hold its power over the medieval nations.

A good reason for drawing a demarcation line between antiquity and the Middle Ages could also be given by referring to the spread of Islam during the decades after the prophet Mohammed's victories in Arabia. During the following decades communication between the civilized nations diminished intellectually as well as geographically. The West became provincial.

When in 800 Charles the Great revived the idea of the Roman Empire, the followers of Mohammed were the masters of the Mediterranean and ruled over almost all of northern Asia, Africa, and the Iberian Peninsula. During the following five centuries Arabic culture was superior to that of the West.[1] Had the Byzantine empire during centuries of heroic fighting not defended Europe against oriental invasions, our so-called Western civilization might have been nipped in the bud. As late as 1529 and 1683, after Constantinople had already fallen (in 1453), Vienna, at that time the capital of the Holy Roman Empire, was besieged by the Turks.

Charles the Great came to the former capital of the world as the representative of the institution that, along with the Church, was destined to organize medieval society. That institution was the feudal system of the Germanic empire. Just as the popes claimed to be the successors of Peter and therefore the spiritual center of Christianity, so the emperors claimed henceforth to be the successors of the Augusti and therefore the leaders of the secular powers of Christendom. It is for this attempt at cooperation between religion and politics that historians have named the Middle Ages "the age of universality." [2]

Indeed, not before the disastrous Thirty Years' War (1618–48) did the peoples of Europe give up the magnificent dream. Certainly it was much of a dream. Since the eleventh century a series of great popes, inspired by the reform movement of the Cluniac order, had reestablished the authority of the papacy over Christendom. Its bearers rejected the tutelage of the emperors, and the cruel struggle broke out by which the two powers eventually forfeited their rights to rule Europe.

If we searched for a deeper motive in the resistance of the Church to the emperors, we could picture the Church as the

1. On the Sarazenic approach to education see E. H. Wilds and K. V. Lottich, *The Foundations of Modern Education*, 3rd ed., New York: Holt, Rinehart and Winston, 1961, pp. 142 ff.
2. See O. Halecki, *The Limits and Divisions of European History*, London: Sheed & Ward, 1950.

defender of the supernational conscience of mankind against the secular ambitions of the state and then draw a line connecting the great popes of the eleventh, twelfth, and thirteenth centuries with minds such as Cicero and Epictetus, who were so deeply concerned with the unity of mankind. The comparison would be faulty, however, because for the medieval Church everything outside Christianity was outside salvation. Its claim to universality was not supported by a truly universal concept of mankind.

However, just as the Church, with its enormous landed property and its soldier-bishops, had become feudal, so the secular rulers had become somewhat Christianized. They were no longer the old barbarian Celtic or Teutonic chieftains. Ideologically at least, sometimes even in practice, they acknowledged that they were "Christian" monarchs "by the grace of God." On the side of the subjects we find already in the Middle Ages the germ of an idea that was to be put into practice during the seventeenth century, namely, that a prince who disobeys the divine commandments may be dethroned by his people. Thus, unforeseen meaning had been present in the encounter between the crosier and the sword.

EDUCATION

The interaction between feudal and religious elements becomes evident also when we pass from the general background to the educational scene. The princes needed the clergy because the members of the clergy were the only ones who were educated and could educate; the clergy needed the princes to safeguard the bases from which they could start their missionary work.

Of the period up to 1000 A.D. we have only a few treatises that could be classified as educational, with Hrabanus Maurus' *On the Instruction of the Clergy* (*De institutione clericorum*) being the most illustrative.[3]

The third part of his treatise deals with education proper. From it and other works of Hrabanus (*c.* 776–856), especially *De universo*, we can gather how the pupils of the monastery school of Fulda in Germany were educated. There existed a *schola exterior* for lay students, probably most of them from the nobility, and a more

---

3. See R. Ulich, *Three Thousand Years of Educational Wisdom*, 2nd ed., Cambridge, Mass.: Harvard Univ. Press, 1954, and *History of Educational Thought*, New York: American Book Co., 1950.

demanding *schola interior* for prospective clerics. The living conditions, though probably typical of those of the earlier Middle Ages, were most primitive. The students slept in their clothes among the monks. It seems, however, that severity of discipline did not exclude kindness and understanding.

The main subject of learning was, of course, religion. Without commitment to the ethics of the Gospel all knowledge was considered meaningless, even full of danger. Concerning the evaluation of pagan literature, Hrabanus quotes the famous words of Augustine to the effect that a good Christian should see the work of God wherever he discovers truth. Of course, selectivity should be exercised in order to sift the chaff from the grain.

As was the tradition, the theological course began with the exposition of the nature of God, of the Creed, and of the Bible. Much value was laid on memorization, but in support of better understanding rather than as an end in itself.

The advanced students read the commentaries of Bede, Alcuin, and their venerated teacher Hrabanus. They also studied the work of some of the church fathers. For the provision of manuscripts the monastery had a special hall for copyists, the *scriptorium,* an institution that was later to become common in the universities.

The secular subjects were taught according to the encyclopedias that, during and after the migration of the nations, transmitted some diluted Hellenistic knowledge to posterity. Rhetoric, according to Hrabanus, should help the pupil to acquire a pleasant form of writing and speaking, especially in homilies. Cicero, whose writings may have been in the library, served as the great pattern. Among other books the students read Quintilian's *Institutions,* lost in later centuries until the humanist Poggio Bracciolini rediscovered it in the fifteenth century at the monastery of St. Gall.

Dialectics was conceived of primarily as a practical art. The logical subtleties of scholasticism did not yet exist; they were not necessary, because Hrabanus' piety was one of simple and unquestioning devotion. Hrabanus thought that dialectics should be cultivated because it would help prospective teachers and preachers to discover logical fallacies and arrive at cogent conclusions before they engaged in the amplification and ornamentation of rhetoric or persuasive oratory.

Among the studies of the quadrivium, Hrabanus ranked arithmetic first because, knowing of the Platonic tradition, he regarded it as "the self-sufficient science" (*disciplina quantitatis secundum se ipsam*) without which geometry, music, and astronomy could not be understood. But geometry shared the honors, for the Lord, besides being an arithmetician, was also a geometrician: *Geometria enim, si fas est dicere, sancta divinitas. (De institutione clericorum)* Of the sciences, such as geology, botany, and mineralogy, Hrabanus speaks with much respect. He felt that they help us to contemplate the miracles of creation. In order to support this view, and in the absence of any real knowledge, he took refuge in mystical explanations as he had learned them from the school of Alcuin, who had relied on a long Christian tradition of allegorical interpretation of Biblical texts.

The total absence of any originality at the time of Hrabanus shows especially in his treatment of history and geography. In history he does not go beyond the Bible, the Jewish historian Josephus, Vergil's *Aeneid,* Origen, Isidore, and the church fathers, while under the title of geography he describes mainly the Holy Land according to Josephus and the report of another Jew, who, perhaps, taught him a bit of Hebrew. Philosophical studies in the modern sense were absent.

What a difference, then, between the attitude of pious acceptance in the ninth century and the intellectual vitality of the second half of the Middle Ages, when we meet the great scholastic philosopher-theologians Albertus Magnus, Thomas Aquinas, and John Duns Scotus, to mention but a few of the great names.

What had happened in the meantime? There are, first of all, material reasons for the change. After centuries during which men had constantly been threatened by Norman invasions, murder and revenge among ruling families, looting and starvation, a degree of security had been achieved. Walled cities with corporate life and commercial intercourse had been built. People could travel about with some safety and could exchange goods in hard and valid money. No longer were isolated monasteries the only places of learning; universities, then called *studia generalia* as distinguished from the more limited *studia,* had begun to attract students and famous scholars from faraway countries.[4] The scholastic universities

---

4. It is impossible to give the exact dates of the origin of all medieval universities, because many of them arose from more or less informal congregations of scholars. At Salerno famous physicians were already teaching during the ninth century, before the university became internationally famous as a medical

were not scientific institutions in the modern sense. Many professors were intensely interested in science, and there was some experimenting, but for lack of modern methods of empirical research progress was slow. Moreover, scholars were under considerable ecclesiastical control. Roger Bacon spent fifteen years in prison; as we know from the life of Galileo, even in the seventeenth century the Roman Inquisition did not tolerate supposedly dangerous ideas.

Nevertheless, as in our times when scientists all over the world communicate with each other in spite of political separations, the scholars of the Middle Ages dared transgress the boundaries of hostile forces. Salerno became the great medical center because its professors studied medical books from Arabic countries and permitted Jews to teach even though, mostly as a consequence of the crusades, they were persecuted all over Europe. The Muslims Averroës and Avicenna and the Jew Maimonides influenced medieval schoolmen to such a degree that at some places the continuity of the Christian dogma was threatened. The theological systems of scholasticism resulted largely from the necessity to provide a coherent structure of thought against the invasion of foreign ideas.

That this could be done was itself due to a foreign influence initially suspected by the Church, the increasing acquaintance with the works of Aristotle. Aristotle provided both the logical instrument and the cognitive substance with which to build a coherent structure of thought, later brought to completion by Thomas Aquinas. The theology of the Catholic Church is still "Thomistic."

In connection with the introduction of Aristotle and the general enrichment of knowledge, the universities could establish a consistent course of studies based on the time-honored trivium for the lower levels and the quadrivium for the advanced levels. The three higher faculties of law, medicine, and theology (the "queen of the

---

center in the eleventh century. At the same time systematic legal studies were being pursued at Bologna, which became the leading school of law. During the twelfth century the University of Paris developed from schools connected with the cathedral on the Ile de la Cité. Oxford and Cambridge can also be traced back to the twelfth century. In the thirteenth and fourteenth centuries there developed in Spain the universities of Valladolid, Seville, and Salamanca. Prague was officially chartered in 1347, Cracow in 1364, Heidelberg in 1385, Cologne in 1388, Erfurt in 1379, Leipzig, a secession from Prague, in 1409, Louvain in 1426, and Budapest in 1475.

sciences") formed the highest story in the edifice of learning. Whereas the students under Hrabanus Maurus at Fulda studied haphazardly what they found in the meager compendia, a student at the acknowledged universities could not graduate as bachelor, master, or doctor (a degree given very rarely) without having gone through a rigid system of courses and examinations.

As evidenced by the never-ending injunctions of the authorities against corruption on the part of both the examiners and the examinees, there must have been loopholes for the wealthy and the influential. Nevertheless, some standards existed. Whatever their defects—and those defects multiplied during the fourteenth and fifteenth centuries—the universities provided the media of exchange for scholars all over Christendom; the same language, Latin, was spoken and the same books were read.

The intellectual ferment provided by the universities grew constantly, even when scholastic philosophy was no longer capable of safeguarding the intellectual and spiritual unity of Europe.

As today, so also in the Middle Ages, the requirements of the universities influenced the minor schools, although a clear division between the various stages of schooling did not yet exist. Except in the urban centers the great majority of people enjoyed no formal schooling. In view of the simplicity of life and production, they would not even have known what to do with it. Nevertheless—often against the opposition of the clergy, which insisted on the right of educational control—the burghers of the larger towns founded schools for their children in which Latin and theology gave way to such practical subjects as letter-writing and bookkeeping. As a result of this development, in the sixteenth and seventeenth centuries we find the beginnings of a school organization roughly comparable to our modern system.

The degree to which the growing complexity of later medieval culture increased the demand for more and better knowledge is amply illustrated by the swelling literature on education,[5] though the education spoken of in this literature was still restricted to the youth of privileged families. The aim of education as expressed

---

5. Hugo of St. Victor, *The Didascalicon of Hugh of Saint Victor*, tr. by J. Taylor, New York: Columbia Univ. Press, 1961 (the first systematic medieval work on education); Vincent of Beauvais, *Speculum majus* (the great compendium of mid-thirteenth century knowledge); and Guilelmus Peraldus, *De eruditione principum*.

in these works reflects the inner continuity of Christian ethics. That aim is essentially the same whether we look into the earlier writings of Hrabanus Maurus, the later writings of John Milton, especially his treatise *Of Education,* or into modern religious literature of the strict observance. Right education, all these documents say, is the means by which fallen man can attain salvation, provided he knows that he needs the grace of God in addition to his own endeavor. For manifold, according to the medieval authors, are the temptations by which Lucifer tries to deflect man from the right path. Some temptations are of a mental nature, such as pride, envy, anger, laziness, and greed; others are of a carnal nature, such as gluttony and lust. The main cause of man's enslavement is ignorance of the good, whereas wisdom opens the way toward virtue and freedom. Wisdom, in turn, can be acquired only through the discipline and practice of study, which in the course of time advances man's nature from a state of crudity to a state of culture.

In regard to methods of teaching, the medieval writers are far ahead of certain modern dabblers in education who believe that "the born teacher" needs only to know his subject and everything else will follow automatically. For example, the chapter on teaching in Vincent of Beauvais' *Liber de eruditione filiorum regalium* (*Book on the Education of Children of the Nobility*) demands that the instructor learn clarity and brevity, that he know how to arouse the learner's interest through right motivation, that he have a sense of moderation and humility, and that he learn to distinguish between that which is significant and that which supports the vanity of erudition. Education should form as well as inform a person, so that he knows how to act in the presence of his superiors as well as of his inferiors, of his friends as well as of his enemies.

The spirit of humaneness that pervades these writings might delude us, causing us to form false opinions about the actual practice. As legal and pictorial sources and the laments of enlightened persons of the time prove, this practice was cruel.

In spite of the admirable example set by the great teacher of agriculture and horticulture, the Benedictine order—whose rules prescribed practical work in addition to prayer and contemplation—the medieval writers inherited from Plato and Aristotle a contempt for the manual arts. Vincent of Beauvais, in his *Speculum majus,* deals at length with the natural creation because it leads us to contemplate the greatness of the Lord, and he reveals what is for his time a considerable knowledge of husbandry, agriculture, and related subjects. But the menial work apparently was left to the plebs. The privileged needed only to know about it.

Nevertheless, the effect of medieval education was by no means restricted to the theoretical. The more civilized interpretation, which we have already mentioned, of the role of the monarch was but one manifestation of the interaction between Christianity and feudalism. It appeared also in attitudes toward war. The early Christians, who took the gospel of love radically, regarded the din of arms as just another sign of the fall of man and the work of the devil.

But during the Middle Ages compromises were made. Christians began to differentiate between war that is just, or war of defense, and war of aggression. From the tenth to the twelfth centuries various synods demanded the Truce of God (*Treuga Dei*). Although not totally effective, it nevertheless mitigated the cruelty of private warfare among the brigand nobles. Gradually the image of the Christian knight arose in contrast to the image of the armed brute. Warriors felt that they gained in dignity and self-prestige by affiliating themselves with Christian ideals. Thus the symbols of knighthood became linked with those of Christianity. The hilt of the sword was likened to the cross; the coats of arms and banners were decorated with sacred signs venerated as talismans, for example, the French oriflamme; and the accolade became a sacred ritual. During his apprenticeship the young knight was told by the chaplain of the castle that he was preparing not only for battle but for entrance into a sacred order of laymen.

The Aristotelian-Christian virtues blended with the old Germanic value of loyalty, and the command to protect the weak produced a phenomenon characteristic of medieval knighthood—the voluntary service of the knight to a venerated woman. This romantic-ascetic sentiment was colored by the Madonna image and the mother motifs that were deeply rooted in the souls of men even before the Christian era. Yet, despite all the false colors mixed into the painting, the French knightly *amour* and the Germanic *minne,* sung by troubadours and minnesingers, helped to transform woman from an object of lust and exploitation into an object of veneration.

Of course, with only a bit of historical knowledge one could write a cruel satire about the continual perversion of sublime ideals into a mere façade—with all the old human vice and vanity, envy, greed, exploitation of the poor, and class struggle behind it. Battalions of bishops and abbots were used for the most unholy purposes. The sword and the cross of the crusaders were stained with the blood of innocent people, and women outside the circle of the privileged were debased just as they had always been.

In spite of all these distortions of professed ideals we still have today the words knightliness, chivalrousness, courtesy, and courtliness not merely as historical denotations, but as connotations and suggestions of desirable conduct. And the only universally accepted designation of a man of desirable behavior, "the gentleman," has its historical origin in the evolution of humane standards developed in the later Middle Ages.

With the rise of cities and the increasing specialization in the production of goods there arose a third educational force besides the clergy and knighthood: the craftsman. As a matter of fact, this force is historically more closely connected with our modern, technological society than are the other two. The medium by which the medieval craftsman transmitted his skill to the next generation was the apprenticeship system. Seven years were required before an apprentice could become a journeyman and help the master as a near-equal in the production of useful articles of daily life as well as carvings, sculptures, and stained-glass windows for the cathedrals, armor for the knights, and jewelry, pewter, and furniture for the rich. In addition to the seven years of apprenticeship spent in the master's household (not always easy years!) in many crafts and in many countries journeymen were required to travel for one or two years before the guild would permit them to settle down as masters. Clearly the artisan might be considered far better educated than either the minor clergy or the average knight, who often was unable to read or write.

Unfortunately, the guilds of the craftsmen, which were a part of the whole medieval corporative order, did not escape the medieval danger of inbreeding and corruption through the abuse of privileges. Just as the higher clergy enriched itself through political maneuvers, and the professors made money out of their examinations, and the fighting vassals threatened the welfare of their nations, so the guildsmen abused their right to determine the length of training and the appointment of their successors. During the sixteenth century cities were thrown into civil war by the rebellion of disappointed workmen—the first unemployed proletariat—and idle

apprentices and journeymen played a major role in the many riots
that, like the frequent revolts of hungry peasants, marked the transition from feudalism to a new social order.

— Yet man's inherent urge for better skills and, through them,
better living could not be killed by social crises. The workshops
of the artisans soon developed into our first centers of advanced
experimentation. Such great minds as Francis Bacon and William
Gilbert knew that they could learn from the artisans. By explaining the causes and the effects of craftsmen's experiences, they led
European thought beyond mere speculation and the trial-and-error
process into the scientific age. But the real pioneers were the
craftsmen.[6]

Suggestions for Class Discussion and Further Investigation

1. What is the significance of the title of this chapter?
2. What changes in education took place between the early and
   late Middle Ages?
3. How do you account for the fact that during the early
   Middle Ages some kings and princes were illiterate although
   most rulers in preceding centuries had been educated well?
4. What were the relative influences of Plato and Aristotle during the first half of the Middle Ages? How did this change
   during the second half? Why?
5. What part did the guilds play in education during the medieval period?

---

6. See C. Hill, "Emergence of the Scientific Method," article II of *Intellectual
   Origins of the English Revolution,* in *The Listener,* 67 (1962), pp. 383–86.

Chapter Four

Humanism and the Renaissance: Education for Individuality

THE BACKGROUND

Both terms—Humanism and Renaissance—are ambiguous. The word humanism suggests the idea of man's interest in man (*homo*). But in every period of history man has been concerned with man. We have no reason to believe that there was less egocentricity in medieval than in modern times. Religion itself made people self-conscious; they were told that, in spite of its transitoriness, life on earth was linked to eternity and that their daily conduct decided their future in the great Beyond.

Nor should we indulge in too simple an equation of more knowledge (which we certainly possess) with more sensitiveness to inner and outer impressions. The mysticism of Meister Eckhart, who lived from about 1260 to 1327, shows a degree of introspection as sublime and profound as that of any later poet or thinker, and the characterizations of individual personalities that Eckhart's contemporary, Dante, achieved in the *Divine Comedy* might put a Balzac or a Dostoevski to shame.

Thus, the difference between the Middle Ages and the Renaissance lies not in the degree of man's self-interest, but in the way in which he relates himself as a person to the universe of which he is a part and, consequently, the way in which he builds his hierarchy of values.

The men whom we may rightly regard as the first representatives of the new mentality were Petrarch and Boccaccio, connected with each other through the bond of friendship. Unlike the medieval schoolmen for whom Latin was primarily a medium of scholarly communication rather than an esthetic creation, Petrarch was enchanted by the beauty of the ancient language. It was for him "literature" in the grand sense of the term. This would not have been the case had not beauty as such excited his sensitive and sensuous mind. He needed poetry for the expression of his strongly emotional personality.

The wonder of genius, of the exceptional and the exalted, dawns on Petrarch. In a letter to the Abbot of St. Benigno, he writes:

> . . . You must recollect that although the delights of poetry are most exquisite, they can be fully understood only by the rarest geniuses, who are careless of wealth and possess a marked contempt for the things of this world, and who are by nature especially endowed with a peculiar elevation and freedom of soul. . . .[1]

Petrarch was an ardent Italian patriot, who in spite of his admiration for Dante could not have written the latter's *Monarchia,* which recommends a universal and supernational Christian empire. Petrarch also loved nature, in which medieval man was but conventionally interested. He dared doubt the infallibility of Aristotle, a dangerous heresy in his time.

Boccaccio, today more widely read than Petrarch, gives us in his *Decameron* the first intimate description of the experiences, loves, and disappointments of mortal—all too mortal—men and women. The moral detachment with which he proceeds is certainly not medieval, nor is his talent for satire, a literary genre that requires distance. Satire was later used with damaging effect by Ulrich von Hutten in his *Letters of the Dark Men,* an attack against monkish ignorance; by Erasmus in his *In Praise of Folly;* and by Sebastian Brant in his widely translated *Ship of Fools (Das Narrenschiff).* These three works contributed more to the cause and the spread of the Reformation than did any other literature except Luther's Ninety-Five Theses.

There is one great passage in the *Decameron* that was used four hundred years later by the German philosopher-poet Gotthold Ephraim Lessing as the central theme of his drama of tolerance, *Nathan the Wise.* It is the story of a rich Jew who, loving his three sons equally, cannot decide to whom to give the sacred ring of wisdom he has inherited from his fathers. He asks a goldsmith to make two other rings indistinguishable from the original. Ever after, no one can tell who has the real ring—whether the Jews, the Muslims, or the Christians. Tolerance to Muslims (along with cruel intolerance to heretical Christians) had already been practiced at the thirteenth-century court of Frederick II. But not until

---

1. J. H. Robinson, *Petrarch,* New York: Putnam, 1898, pp. 166 *ff.*

the Renaissance could people write and read about it, at least in certain places.

Both Humanism and the Renaissance have been connected with the notion of the Revival of Learning. A revival of learning had already taken place, as we have seen, in the twelfth and thirteenth centuries; the admiration of ancient wisdom was as unswerving then as in the Renaissance. But that wisdom was used differently; it served mainly theological purposes, whereas the Humanists tried to enter into its original spirit. With Poggio as the leader, they discovered dozens of precious manuscripts, among them Quintilian's *Institutes of Oratory,* dusty and forgotten in the storerooms of old monasteries. Johann Reuchlin, born shortly before Poggio's death in 1459, risked the persecution of the Inquisition for his interest in the Hebrew language and its literary documents and had to be defended by Erasmus. Erasmus himself was equally great as a translator and interpreter of the New Testament, as the editor of an enormous volume of Christian literature, as a satirist and author of books on politics and education, as an influential letterwriter, and as adviser of the mighty. A truly liberal Christian, he showed his alienation from Rome even in the hour of his death by refusing to ask for a priest. His fortune he bequeathed for charitable purposes outside the Church. But he felt equally foreign to the vehemence of Luther, who accused him of timidity. Was it perhaps a sign of greater courage to stand aloof from the fighting parties?

While in England, Erasmus lived at the home of Sir Thomas More, Humanist, statesman, and author of the famous *Utopia,* a satire of serious intent in which he recommended a national system of education and the rule of work for all. More showed his final greatness in the martyrdom he suffered for refusing to take an oath that would have given supremacy in religious matters to his absolutist monarch Henry VIII.

This monarch was a complex mixture of Humanist, scoundrel, and national leader, a type of personality that would have been an anachronism in the Middle Ages. Actually, Henry resembled Pope Alexander VI (Rodrigo Borgia) and his son Cesare Borgia more than he did the northern Humanists. For the men of the north found their fulfillment less in the explorations and adventures of secularity than in scholarship and a most personal confrontation with the divine. In Italy, too, the dialogue between man and God assumed new forms. There Michelangelo struggled like a Titan with

the powers of the Creation, and Pico della Mirandola expressed his
Neo-Platonic mysticism in his unforgettable *Oration on the Dignity
of Man*.[2]

Nevertheless, the spirit of Latin Catholicism, together with the
power of the Church, was strong enough to keep the divergent elements under one roof. In contrast, for reasons spiritual as well as
political, in the north the change was more complete. To be sure,
the Reformation spread also into France and the south of Europe,
and Calvinism found a permanent abode in Geneva. On the whole,
however, Protestantism became more a Germanic than a Latin
phenomenon.

If there is such a difference between the Italian Renaissance and
the northern Reformation, how can a common denominator be
found? What do the elegance of Petrarch and Boccaccio, the heroism of Michelangelo, the hedonism of Lorenzo Medici, and the
philosophical conversations of his Academy [3] have in common with
the transcendentalist furor of the northern reformers? It would, of
course, be easy to say "nothing." Yet the two movements belong
together in one fundamental respect.

In both movements man is no longer embedded; rather, he feels
confronted. Generalizations, of course, are dangerous. But when we
speak of a Renaissance person, we refer to a man who no longer
believes in the efficacy of rituals prescribed by an ecclesiastical institution, a man who is no longer satisfied with the logical subtleties
of Thomistic theology. Rather, he considers religion an inner experience which he cannot devolve on anyone else. This applies not
only to the Protestants, but also to their most radical enemy,
Ignatius of Loyola. For, despite his radical subjection to the papal
Church, Ignatius wrote his *Spiritual Exercises* as a testimony of
one of man's most intense occupations with the Divine. Something
similar could be said of Francis of Sales, author of the *Introduction
to the Devout Life,* and of the Carmelite nun Theresa of Ávila.
To them all the transcendental was not real unless it became also
immanent.

While discussing the culture of the Renaissance we should not
forget its social and economic background. The cities had become

---

2. G. Pico della Mirandola, *Oration on the Dignity of Man,* tr. by A. R. Capo-
   nigri, Chicago: Regnery, 1956.
3. P. A. Kristeller, *The Philosophy of Marsilio Ficino,* tr. by V. Conant, New
   York: Columbia Univ. Press, 1943.

safer and richer; the invention of movable type for printing had completely changed the older forms of communication and thus made possible the participation of a wider group of people in the affairs of man. The experiences of a few became now the concern of the many.

The consequences of the individualistic breakthrough of the Renaissance reached far beyond religion into political and social life as well. The present distinction between totalitarian and free countries, between "subjects" and "citizens," and between children as mere objects of culture and as participants in that culture can be traced back to this era. However, we should not exaggerate. For, unfortunately, the multiplicity of denominations and loyalties by no means guaranteed freedom of religious conscience within the arising individual domains of Christendom. It took some centuries for this to be achieved, and in some countries it is still in continuous jeopardy. Directly after the Reformation the cruel principle *cuius regio, eius religio* (as the prince, so the religion) determined the policy of governments in ecclesiastical matters. Hapless minorities were forced either to be converted or to be tortured or expelled. Thus one can hardly speak of any immediate improvement of the religious situation throughout Europe.

EDUCATION

With the Renaissance, absolutism, or the centralization of power in the hands of the government, began to replace the obsolete order of loosely interrelated corporations that was characteristic of the Middle Ages. Like the townspeople, the new governments disliked the monopoly of the Church and especially the practices of the Inquisition, which handed condemned men over to the secular arm to do the work of the executioner.

Both princes and cities looked with envy at the enormous ecclesiastical property holdings, which often amounted to one-fourth or more of a country's area. "Die tote Hand" (the dead hand), men said of the Church when they spoke of economic matters, sometimes even spiritual matters. The princes and the cities were also interested in ending the feuds of the nobility. This group had become impoverished as a result of the devaluation of landed property and had lost its raison d'être after the growth of standing armies equipped with firearms.

In order to provide law and defense, the absolutist princes needed the rights of legislation, jurisdiction, and taxation. They preferred bureaucrats trained in monarchical Roman law to free men sitting in corporate council, and they needed a more literate population to carry out their political and mercantile plans.

These changes in the intellectual and social setting could not fail to affect the educational scene. In regard to the control of the universities there had been rivalries between monarchs and popes almost from the beginning. With the rise of absolutism during the fifteenth century the balance went in favor of the states. Intellectually they represented the more progressive element in the rising conflicts between clergy and laymen. Politically, however, they were questionable friends, because they disliked the transnationality of the old centers of learning. What they gave with one hand they took back with the other. When, for example, King Louis XI of France, the great proponent of state centralization, ordered in 1474 that the rector of the University of Paris should not come from any other nation than the French, he abolished one of the finest prerogatives of medieval learning. One can, however, understand Louis' irritation over the monopolistic abuses practiced by this once great and proud institution.[4]

When the countries that embraced the Reformation severed their schools from the Catholic Church and confiscated its property, they assumed, along with the financing of the schools, substantial control over them. Under secular influence the scope of the curriculum was widened and humanistic and practical subjects were included. One should not, however, infer that the secularization of administration brought with it greater freedom of religious instruction. On the contrary, the heat of the theological differences caused an intensification of dogmatic instruction. For then as in later times it was understood that lasting victory could not be assured without the indoctrination of the youth.

However, before the religious conflicts forced Western Europe into a rigorous reevaluation of its religious tradition, the Italian Humanists were permitted to express their educational goals freely. They did so in a constantly swelling number of writings. Paolo Vergerio wrote *On Good Morals and Liberal Studies* (1402); Leon-

---

4. See H. Rashdall, *The Universities of Europe in the Middle Ages*, ed. by F. M. Powicke and A. B. Emden, Oxford: Clarendon Press, 1936, vol. 1, p. 430.

ardo Bruni, *On Studies and Letters* (1415); Leone Battista Alberti, *On the Family* (in the 1430's); Aeneas Silvius (Pope Pius II), *On the Education of Youth* (1445); Battista Guarino, *On Teaching and Learning* (1459); and Maffeo Vegio, *On the Liberal and Moral Education of Children* (about 1450).[5]

To describe the Humanist approach to learning we may best use the term "worldliness." Of course, as educators the Humanists would not and could not criticize Christianity. In fact, many of them belonged to the clergy, which itself had become extremely liberal. It did not matter that they expressed in unambiguous words their contempt for the old scholastic studies and the universities as a whole. Indeed, men who exalted genius, originality, the arts, and the beauty of genteel living could find no pleasure in the scholastic emphasis on pedestrian logic and on arguments one could just as well prove as disprove. Some of the Italian Humanists studied at universities, but they never returned; like many great minds of the seventeenth and eighteenth centuries, they placed no value on teaching at universities that lagged behind the spirit of the time. Instead, the enlightened minds of the Renaissance preferred the new academies, where they could freely discuss poetry, philosophy, and science.

This shift of values expressed itself also in statements about the aims that should regulate the upbringing of youth. The influence of Quintilian is apparent everywhere. The seven liberal arts still served as the general framework for advanced education, though the study of literature, neglected by the scholastics, now played a prominent role. As one accepted religion, so one accepted also the Christian virtues of faith, hope, and charity, which had been loosely combined with the Greek virtues of wisdom, fortitude, temperance, and justice. Now the Humanists added virtues alien to the medieval tradition, such as fame, glory for oneself and the family, patriotism, and excellence in the service of prince and country. The Latin of the scholastics was ridiculed; once again Cicero became the great exemplar of style.

Indeed, Cicero would have been horrified could he have listened to a typical medieval university discussion, provided he could have understood what they were talking about. One could perhaps have

---

5. For a more detailed description see R. Ulich, *History of Educational Thought, op. cit.*, p. 108.

persuaded him that a language can survive only if it serves as a medium for expressing what has to be expressed. That was exactly the case with the Latin of the medieval schoolmen. In all their disrespect for linguistic purity, they had made Latin the means of international communication and of sacred and worldly poetry. *Dies irae* (ascribed to Thomas of Celano, disciple and biographer of Francis of Assisi) is one of the most powerful Christian hymns, while the often very frivolous Latin poetry of the vagrant scholars excels through its vitality and lyrical rhythm. What the Humanists gained in purity they lost in freedom of expression. The unprejudiced Erasmus saw this clearly when he satirized the Ciceronians in his *Ciceronianus, or, A Dialogue on the Best Style of Speaking.*[6] Furthermore, when the Humanists revived classical Latin, man's most heroic feelings and his deepest emotions had already been expressed in the vernacular. Dante had employed the *vulgare* in his *Divine Comedy,* as had Petrarch in his *Canzoniere* and Boccaccio in his *Decameron.*

One of the most valuable sources of information on the educational ideals of Italian Humanism is the treatise *On Education* by the Italian cardinal Jacopo Sadoleto.[7] It contains all the characteristics of Humanist education mentioned so far, but it deals somewhat more extensively than other writings with religion. Parents and teachers, the cardinal says, should plant the fear of God early in the souls of the young. Nevertheless, the pagan authors and their philosophy are given such a preference that one of the author's friends, the English Archbishop Reginald Pole, asked him whether he had not mistaken "the times of Plato, Aristotle and Cicero" for the time when "God and His Son have given us a much better haven for our souls." [8]

Here is the decisive difference between the Italian Humanists and those of the north. As we have already indicated, the latter were less mundane. Moreover, they did not have the courts of the Medici and the Este to support them. They hoped to reform the universities from within. However, even they agreed that scholas-

6. Erasmus, *Ciceronianus,* tr. by I. Scott, New York: Teachers College, Columbia Univ., 1908.
7. J. Sadoleto, *On Education,* tr. by E. T. Campagnac and E. Forbes, Oxford: Oxford Univ. Press, 1946.
8. R. Pole, *Epistola No. 13. Venetiis. November, 1532,* in *Epistolarum R. Poli collectio,* ed. by G. Quirini, Brescia: Italy. 1744–57, vol. 1, p. 399.

ticism, Aristotelianism, and the whole medieval curriculum had become obsolete.

No one could have been more outspoken in this respect than Erasmus, the Protestant reformer Ulrich von Hutten, and even the loyal Catholic philosopher Juan Luis Vives, author of *On the Corruption of the Arts* (*De causis corruptarum artium*).

The northern Humanists, of course, did not spurn the inspiration that could come from the ancients. They even studied Hebrew works, which, except in rare cases, the Italians did not cultivate. Martin Luther expressed the difference clearly when the Humanist poets of the University of Erfurt accused him of neglecting the new learning. He fully appreciated it, he said, and young people should cultivate their minds by studying "poetry and rhetoric"; but, foremost and essentially, the ancient languages were for him the languages of the Old and New Testaments and of the church fathers.

> And let us be sure of this: we shall not long preserve the Gospel without the languages. The languages are the sheath in which this sword of the Spirit is contained.[9]

Suggestions for Class Discussion and Further Investigation

1. Contrast the Renaissance view of man's relation to the universe with the view most widely held during the Middle Ages.
2. Examine several different definitions of the words "humanism" and "humanities." What conclusions can you draw?
3. What has been the long-range influence of Humanism on education? What is its influence today?
4. How did the decline of Latin and the rise of the vernaculars affect education throughout Europe? Is it fortunate or unfortunate that Latin is no longer the common language of scholarship?
5. What was the effect of the Inquisition on education?
6. What are the founding dates and the geographical locations of the ten oldest European universities? What conclusions can you draw?

---

9. M. Luther, *To the Councilmen of All Cities in Germany That They Establish and Maintain Christian Schools*, in *Works*, ed. by H. E. Jacobs, Philadelphia: Holman, 1915–32, vol. 4, p. 114.

7. Why did the establishment of universities precede the wide-spread development of elementary and secondary schools?
8. Do you agree that the emphasis during the Renaissance was on education for individuality, as the title of this chapter implies?

Chapter Five

The Seventeenth Century: Education for Communion

THE BACKGROUND

Our journey through the various stages of Western culture has shown us several trends in educational systems: the Greek interest in reason, the Roman sense of order, the Jewish concern with the Covenant, the Christian aspiration for saintliness, the medieval trend toward hierarchy, and the Renaissance longing for individual self-fulfillment.

Although one particular predisposition dominated in each period, the great achievements of the past never disappeared, and although the cumulative quality of progressing cultures led in some minds to magnificent syntheses, it brought conflict and confusion to others. This was especially evident in the seventeenth century, for that was the century in which the overwhelming heritage of the past met head-on with a similarly overwhelming body of new ideas.

Even more than in earlier times the ancient languages were cultivated in the advanced schools of Catholics and Protestants. The scholars still wrote in Latin. The greatest jurists of the time, such as the Dutchman Hugo Grotius and the Spaniard Francisco Suárez, were also classicists and theologians.

The Council of Trent (1545–63) had bound Catholic philosophy to the medieval theology of Thomas Aquinas, and even Protestant divines found some value in the scholastic tradition, which they had repudiated at the beginning of the Reformation.

Among the laymen, less familiar with the subtleties of theology, the medieval mystics were widely read. Finally, the style of the Renaissance, often exaggerated into baroque, continued in the arts and in poetry, and so did its cult of personality.

So conscious did the seventeenth century become of the abundance of legacies from the past that there appeared a considerable number of encyclopedias in which the authors tried—almost in moods of despair—to channel the overflow of scholarship into some kind of *pansophia,* or universal system of knowledge.

It is one of the most amazing phenomena in history that the seventeenth century, embarrassed as it was by its intellectual riches, was at the same time a century of great calamity for large parts of Europe. For this was the century of the Thirty Years' War (1618–48). Germany has never recovered from its wounds. The population was decimated; hordes of homeless children swarmed over the villages; the proud and freedom-loving cities were destroyed, and the gap between the social classes widened; the last hopes for European unity were buried when the German realm split into hundreds of ridiculously small, absolutist principalities in which there was no opportunity for common enterprise or the development of political wisdom. Switzerland and the Netherlands became independent of Germany. The country ceased to be a nation and became instead an enormous battlefield on which its own princes joined foreign powers in the business of dividing the population and persecuting inhabitants of other faiths.

People suffered everywhere. When Rubens explained the allegoric meaning of his painting "The Horrors of War" (which was to the age of baroque more or less what Picasso's "Guernica" is to our time), he referred to one of the figures as follows:

> That grief stricken woman, clothed in black, with torn veil, robbed of all her jewels and other ornaments, is the unfortunate Europe who, for so many years now, has suffered plunder, outrage, and misery.[1]

Yet there was not only an overwhelming heritage, both good and evil, from the past. There was also a bewildering influx of the new. Edward Herbert, the first Baron of Cherbury, became known as the "Father" of English deism, which established a "natural" as well as the "revealed" religion. His contemporary, René Descartes, believed that he could base a philosophical system exclusively on rational principles. All over Europe the leading minds approached the problems of nature and man, no longer deductively as in earlier times, but inductively by means of observation and experiment. The modern scientific and technological era had begun.

The impact of the empirical sciences on the minds of the seventeenth and eighteenth centuries was truly revolutionary. Nature

---

1. P. P. Rubens, *Letters,* tr. and ed. by R. S. Magurn, Cambridge, Mass.: Harvard Univ. Press, 1958. p. 408.

was suddenly deprived of its human elements. One could no longer describe it as the manifestation of God or as the "hunting ground of the devil," or interpret it according to the ends and purposes which man found within himself. Instead, it was discovered that nature had a causality of its own. The earth to which God had sent His own Son was—as Copernicus had shown—by no means the center of the universe. Now Aristotle became just another wise, but nevertheless erring, mortal, because the newly invented telescope proved that he and his followers had tried to explain a world they had never really seen.

The key word of the new understanding was "method." (The term comes from the Greek and means "the right way.") It meant that one should not deduce statements from preconceived notions with the results already in mind, but should do as Galileo, Boyle, Huygens, Newton, and others did. Look first at the unit before explaining the whole; check and recheck the outcome. Then one will see the relation between right approach and right result, or wrong approach and wrong result. The effect of that attitude on modern schooling need not be emphasized. The relatively peaceful revolution it has brought about surpasses all the violent religious and political revolutions of earlier centuries both in magnitude and depth.

All this was not entirely new. As we have seen, the craftsmen had always been experimentalists, though they had developed no adequate theory. Medicine at the University of Salerno and natural philosophy at the University of Padua had had an empirical direction. In 1543 there had been published a work by the Belgian physician Andreas Vesalius, *On the Fabric of the Human Body* (*De humani corporis fabrica*), which established the modern science of anatomy. But if the emperor Charles V had not protected Vesalius, he might have become the victim of the Inquisition. The Inquisition was already in pursuit of the Spanish physician, Michael Servetus, who, however, because of his doubts about the trinity of the Godhead became instead the victim of the Protestant grand inquisitor, Calvin. But the new design of research appeared at too many places to be put down. The scientists were joined by the philosophers, of whom we will speak in the next chapter, and although some of them were more speculatively than empirically minded, they all were groping after the right method of thinking. Thus, despite the perseverance of the old dualism in Christian theology as well as in philosophy (especially in Descartes), there emerged new concepts of the relation between mind and cosmos. Man, it was thought, could not understand the laws of nature so well if there did not exist a close affinity between those laws and the human person—indeed, if man himself were not a part of nature. The universe became "one." In some minds the new attitude created a materialistic philosophy that had been lost since early antiquity ("all life is matter"); in others it created deism ("God created the machinery and then withdrew to let it run of its own momentum"); in yet others it created a form of idealistic or religious pantheism, a new sense of communion between man and the universe.

JOHN AMOS COMENIUS

The genius who introduced into education this religious spirit of communion between man and the creation was John Amos Comenius, the last bishop of the Moravian and Bohemian Brethren. Like other great men of his time, he lived in the twilight between the old and the new, between ideas that remind us of the Middle Ages and ideas that announce the coming of the Enlightenment.

Of references to antiquity, his writings are full. He knew the church fathers and the scholastics; the mystical pantheism of the Renaissance had touched him; his religious tradition went back to Wycliffe, Huss, and Luther, though these men did not have his interest in looking at the world as a whole, as a union of nature and spirit. He knew the writings of Francis Bacon. In 1642 he met Descartes, whom he admired, though he disagreed with a rationalism that seemed to exclude the divine source of inspiration. Science, or "method," was for the profoundly pious Comenius, exiled from his home country by the Catholic monarchy of the Spanish Hapsburgs, not merely a matter of cool and critical reflection, but another way through which the Almighty reveals his infinite kindness and order.

This faith was particularly apparent in the Moravian's concept of "light," as expressed in a letter to the English Royal Society.[2] Light, for Comenius, was not merely a physical, but a spiritual qual-

---

2. J. A. Comenius, *The Way of Light*, tr. by E. T. Campagnac, Liverpool: Univ. Press of Liverpool, 1938.

ity, similar to the Neo-Platonic *logos*. If understood as a metaphor this term is persuasive. Even in ordinary language we say, "I see the light," and we use the words "bright" and "dark" in an intellectual sense. However, metaphor contributes nothing to exact knowledge, as Comenius could have learned from the Dutch scientists who had already made some of the first optical experiments. Two years after Comenius' death, Newton in 1672 sent his first report on color experiments to the Royal Society, and in 1690 Huygens published his work on the fundamental laws of optics in his *Treatise on Light (Traité de la lumière)*.

Nevertheless, Comenius' *Via lucis* testifies to the author's conviction that the future of mankind would be enlivened by the advancement of science. If we are to judge his mysticism understandingly, we must not forget that at his time the dividing line between mysticism and science was not so sharply drawn as it is today. Newton himself included in his *Philosophiae naturalis principia mathematica* a mystical treatise on "The System of the World" (*De systemate mundi*)—though only after some persuasion. The human world is still full of myth; without it, mankind might be poorer.

Underlying Comenius' treatise, *The Way of Light,* is his belief that the divine order shines through the whole world. Consequently, if the teacher obeys these laws, which are universally valid, then he will achieve certain results. Moreover, he will achieve the same results with every pupil. Differences of talent (*differentiae ingenii*) will play no role. Each person can learn as well as everyone else. This belief in the omnipotence of methodical science is, of course, naive; it was, nevertheless, shared by such great thinkers as Bacon and Descartes. Thus it was in the temper of the time that Comenius announced his main pedagogical work the *Great Didactic (Didactica magna)* with the following words:

> The Great Didactic Setting forth The Whole Art of Teaching all Things to all Men or A certain Inducement to found such Schools in all the Parishes, Towns, and Villages of every Christian Kingdom, that the entire Youth of both Sexes, none being excepted, shall Quickly, Pleasantly, & Thoroughly Become learned in the Sciences, pure in Morals, trained to Piety, and in this manner instructed in all things necessary for the present and for the future life, in which, with respect to everything that is suggested, Its Fundamental Principles are set forth from the essential nature of the matter. Its Truth is proved by examples from the several mechanical arts, Its Order is clearly set

forth in years, months, days, and hours, and, finally, An Easy and Sure Method is shown, by which it can be pleasantly brought into existence. [3]

Comenius tried to confirm his educational insights, won as a teacher and a loving observer of nature, by resorting to this same mechanical concept of the inner unity of all things—specifically, by pointing out the similarities between the breeding habits of animals and the upbringing of youth. Comenius deserves to be mentioned by our historians of science as one of the intuitive forerunners of Darwin, for in the *Great Didactic* he utters the monumental sentence: "Nature knits everything together in continuous combination." [4]

Despite its obvious defects, the *Great Didactic* is a milestone in the history of education. Comenius perceived more clearly than any of his predecessors the significance of method and order in the process of instruction. Before him, only the cryptic Wolfgang Ratke had conceived of a school reform based on the natural aptitudes and experiences of the child, but his experiment at the Thuringian town of Köthen failed. Nevertheless, Comenius was indebted to Ratke, and it may be partly due to that debt that he said in Chapter XVII of the *Great Didactic:*

> Following the footsteps of nature we find that the process of education will be easy
> I. If it begin early, before the mind is corrupted.
> II. If the mind be duly prepared to receive it.
> III. If it proceed from the general to the particular.
> IV. And from what is easy to what is more difficult.
> V. If the pupil be not overburdened by too many subjects.
> VI. And if progress be slow in every case.
> VII. And if the intellect be forced to nothing to which its natural bent does not incline it, in accordance with each age and with the right method.
> VIII. If everything be taught through the medium of the senses.
> IX. And if the use of everything taught be continually kept in view.
> X. If everything be taught according to one and the same method.

Certainly, if slavishly applied, these rules could become merely another didactical straitjacket. Yet if their spirit is understood, they make for good teaching. Surprisingly enough, Comenius did

---

3. J. A. Comenius, *Great Didactic,* tr. and ed. by M. W. Keatinge, London: Macmillan, 1910, Part II, p. 155. The Czech original, completed around 1632, was published in Prague in 1849; a Latin translation was published in Amsterdam in 1657 (see Part I, p. 14).

4. *Ibid.,* ch. xviii, 8th Principle.

not apply his rules in his own textbooks. Only in his *The World in Pictures (Orbis sensualium pictus)* did he combine the learning of Latin with the learning of the things indicated by the words, as was done in some fashion in the later primers.

Far beyond education proper, the Moravian bishop is known for his concern with the progress of mankind as a whole. This concern was the natural result of several ideas that had converged in his sensitive mind. Although he could not conceive of man's final salvation except through Christ, he had discovered the essential and universal element that emerges whenever a person transcends dogmatism and sees the deep unity in the religious experiences of humanity. There is some likelihood of truth in the story that Comenius was invited by the New England Puritans to become the president of the newly founded Harvard College. Had he accepted, his employers might soon have suggested that he return to Europe—for, although his interest in science might have been appreciated by one of their leading ministers, Cotton Mather, who in this respect was far ahead of his fellow citizens, Comenius' tendency toward pantheism would have seemed heresy to the dualistically minded New Englanders. Nor would their insistence on predestination have harmonized with Comenius' metaphysics of light. He might even have shared the fate of the Quakers who dared import their idea of the Light of Christ into the Puritan New Jerusalem.

It certainly added to Comenius' sympathy for the cause of humanity that he had suffered from persecution and war. The evil of persecution, perhaps all evil, he thought, results when man fails to extricate himself from the absolutist tendencies in his ego —in other words, when he is afraid of his own freedom. Thus, despite all his disappointments, Comenius was never really defeated. At a time of extreme intolerance, he was the apostle of tolerance.

> For there is inborn in human nature a love of liberty—for liberty man's mind is convinced that it is made—and this love can by no means be driven out: so that wherever and by whatever means it feels that it is being hemmed in and impeded, it cannot but seek a way out and declare its own liberty.[5]

Convinced that with knowledge the wisdom of man would increase, he believed in the future of great organizations that would

---

5. J. A. Comenius, *The Way of Light, op. cit.,* p. 18.

help mankind toward peace, unity, and greater happiness. The reality, even the idea, of a Holy Roman Empire was gone forever; man had to look for new means of survival. For Comenius that search should eventuate in a great community where each member would help the others on the road toward salvation, away from hatred, error, and misery. Thus, he demanded a world parliament in which "Learning, Religion and Government may be brought to certain immutable principles or bases." He asked also for "universal books, universal schools, a universal college" and, like Luis Vives and Bacon, for a "universal language." [6]

Certainly much of what Comenius demanded was utopian. As in his various attempts to achieve a unified system of education and a *pansophia,* he was too much impressed by the idea of the universal applicability of methodical procedure to all the problems of mankind. He thus overlooked the necessity for, and the productiveness of, variety. Yet the utopia he described was—in contrast to others presented at a time when this genre of thinking abounded— not a mere playing with the impossible but an expression of the highest ethical strivings of man.

Education will never be a science in the strict sense of the word, for it is concerned with the freedom of the person and his society. Because it is related to the natural and social sciences on the one hand, and to the humanities on the other, it is too diversified and multilateral to be pressed into the rigidity of a typical discipline. For that very reason it needs continuous self-examination as to its proper subjects, its methods, its ends, and its practices. It is to Comenius' credit that he paved the way toward this goal for the first time in the Christian era.

In order to illustrate the significance of the seventeenth century for modern civilization and the place of Comenius in the culture of his time, we must mention the work of two other men along with that of Comenius. They are Grotius and Spinoza. The Netherlands was then what Switzerland and the United States were to become later—the refuge of free minds escaping intolerance at home. In the case of Grotius, however, even the Netherlands failed him, for he was thrown into prison as a religious dissenter. And Spinoza was a solitary even in his own Jewish community.

---

6. *Ibid.,* pp. 8 *ff.* See also J. A. Comenius, *Panegersia, excitatorium universale,* Amsterdam, 1666, ch. xi, 19.

Both Grotius and Spinoza possessed an encyclopedic knowledge which they wanted to use for synthesis rather than for further division; both were steeped in the philosophical and philological wisdom of the past (with Spinoza adding the Judaic tradition to the typically Christian); both attempted to reveal the essence of religion rather than insisting on its accidental accretions. Both—Grotius in international law and Spinoza in philosophy—were searching for new methods of bringing order into a world of crisis. Both desired to help the cause of tolerance and freedom (Spinoza, in his *Tractatus Theologico-Politicus*, introduced the phrase *libertas philosophandi* to define the condition of human progress), and both believed that the unity of mankind could be accomplished only by an increasing understanding of the "laws of nature." This was a heroic program, indeed, perhaps forever beyond achievement. Yet it contained the directive vision the loss of which would mean the loss of hope for a better civilization.

JEAN-JACQUES ROUSSEAU

One can hardly imagine personalities more different in character and background than those of the Moravian bishop Comenius and the Swiss Jean-Jacques Rousseau. Comenius was firmly rooted in the tradition of his church despite its dispersion. He was a savant who developed his ideas steadily and believed in his mission in spite of a life of wandering. And he was one of the few men of his time who were able to combine mysticism with rationality and tolerance for other opinions. The fact that he fell prey to a false prophetess was nothing unusual at a time when many of his contemporaries burned witches and believed in miracles.

By contrast, Rousseau was a genius without roots who would have wandered about even if he had not been persecuted. He was enchanted with himself even in the shameless recording of his adventures. He was ambitious and proud and at the same time tortured by feelings of inferiority, attracted by the life of the powerful whom at the same time he despised, and helpless without the support of women whom he easily betrayed. Yet it was exactly this twisted kind of existence that caused him to raise the cry that resounded all over Europe: "Retournez à la nature!"

The reasons for the amazing divergence of opinion about the educational work of Rousseau—some praise it as extravagantly as others condemn it—lie in the various interpretations of the concept of "nature." Indeed, this concept has been one of the most ambiguous in the history of ideas. To the naturalistically inclined it has been all that is healthy and unspoiled—the creative source, the genuine order, the paradise. For the dualists, especially those with an ascetic tendency, it has symbolized the impulsive, the source of sin and lust, the pagan, "the flesh and the world," the way to hell.

Thus, for the young Goethe and his friends of the *Sturm und Drang* (storm and stress) Rousseau was the apostle of genius, whereas for John Wesley, the father of Methodism, as for most clergymen of his time, he was an abomination, a misanthrope, a cynic, a coxcomb, and an infidel.[7]

We should remember that the philosopher Kant, whom no one can accuse of lack of critical judgment, spoke of Rousseau with a sense of gratitude:

> He [Rousseau] has freed me from my illusions [about the supreme value of pure scholarship]. He has taught me to respect mankind, and I would consider myself much less useful than the ordinary worker, if I did not believe that this very insight could justify all my other thinking and help me to do my share in the restoration of the rights of man.[8]

In more recent times, Leo Tolstoy acknowledged Rousseau's influence when he arrived at his personal interpretation of the teaching of Christ.

Some parents, mostly of the higher classes, took Rousseau's gospel of nature so seriously that they endangered the health of their children by excessive attempts to strengthen their bodies. Other parents, mostly of the solid middle class, considered him immoral. But if seemingly insignificant things may indicate the significant, since the time of Rousseau children have not been forced into the formal clothes of adults (as in the paintings of Van Dyck and Watteau) but have been permitted to move their limbs freely.

Actually, nature was for Rousseau much more than mere freedom from coercion. One has but to read the first pages of his chief educational work, *Émile, ou Traité de l'éducation*, in order to see that he did not confuse nature with license. He accused of license those who dared to spoil and deform nature by arbitrary and

---

7. J. Wesley, February 3, 1770, entry in *Journal*, New York: Dutton, 1907.
8. I. Kant, *Fragmente aus dem Nachlass*, in *Sämtliche Werke*, ed. by G. Hartenstein, Leipzig: Meiner, 1873, vol. 8, p. 322.

false conventions. By "nature" he meant something extremely precious, that center of creativeness in the human person which enables him to become disciplined and civilized without losing his identity and his naturalness. Therefore, in a letter to a young man who sought his advice, he could say, "Rentrez dans votre cœur." In other words, the one who examines his heart, or his soul, or his conscience, will also find his nature.

We all can experience the meaning of these abstractions in concrete human situations. We meet persons in whose presence we have a sense of comfort because they have harmonized the impositions of civilization with their inner truth. They have not lost their authenticity. How different they are from persons whose achievements we respect but in whom there still appears the strain that has made them what they are. They are not yet themselves.

Needless to say, even a balanced and natural person goes through conflicts, but these help him to mature without too many branches cracking in the storms of life. Sigmund Freud has seen this clearly in his maturity principle. If the id, or the dark force that lives in each of us, is still unabsorbed by the ego, the ego will rebel against society. The immature or the sick person is the one in whom the fighting forces have not been integrated.

This was the case with Rousseau. He knew from his own experience that culture is not nature and nature is not culture, but that culture is not real culture if nature has been destroyed. This is the central theme of *Émile*. The tutor leads the child not only through experiences he enjoys, but also through those that hurt. Wisdom lies in turning harm into insight. We will see in a later discussion how Pestalozzi, another Swiss, used the same principle, under the name of "organic development," as the basis for his own educational theory and practice, but more wisely than Rousseau. It was the power of Rousseau's language that gave voice to the protest against the artificiality of the baroque and rococo culture of Louis XIV and his imitators.

Rousseau aroused the most heated controversy among his contemporaries through his opinions on religious education—an outgrowth not merely of his educational views, but also of his deistic philosophy as he expressed it sentimentally in a part of the *Émile*, the "confession of a Savoyard vicar" ("Profession de foi du vicaire savoyard"). In accordance with his conviction that nothing should be imposed on a young mind for which it is not ready, Rousseau wished to have the mention of God delayed until adolescence, for not before this age does a person ask metaphysical questions.

Here, as with the concept of nature, everything depends on what is meant by religion and religious education. If one knows something about the typical religious instruction in Rousseau's time—instruction that was mainly occupied with memorizing the catechism of a particular denomination—then one may well sympathize with his position. Pestalozzi, who felt that piety should be instilled at a very early age, also condemned such instruction, and so did the famous Protestant theologian Schleiermacher. Even today thousands of men and women have warped conceptions of religion because they remember the clumsy indoctrination to which they were exposed in their youth.

If, on the other hand, one means by religious education the gradual awakening in the child of a sense of reverence for the great wonder of existence, then one could say that the education of Rousseau's Émile was fundamentally religious, because it prepared the mind of the young for ever-new questions about the depth and meaning of life.

But then there opens up a third proposition, and this is the one that conservative teachers of religion can use against their critics. Are the life and mind of a child not formed by many impressions which he cannot yet fully understand? Entering first into his subconscious, they may emerge into the conscious with growing maturity. They may form the person even if they remain in the subconscious. What, then, could be more important than to plant early the seeds of a religiously directed conscience?

Whatever the answer, Rousseau succeeded in arousing teachers to struggle with an issue that should not be left to mere convention.

As we have already seen, important educational ideas reflect on politics, and vice versa. For Rousseau a body politic that would correspond to his conception of human health could only be one in which respect was shown for the "Laws of Nature and of Nature's God"—as Thomas Jefferson, also a deist, wrote in The Declaration of Independence.

The principal work in which Rousseau formulated his political philosophy is his *Social Contract (Du contrat social)*. Its thesis is that government should result not from divine right but from the consensus of the ruler and the ruled. This thesis had already been forcefully advanced by the French Huguenots at the end of the sixteenth century in the *Vindiciae contra tyrannos* (1579) attributed to Hubert Languet, by Spinoza in his *Tractatus Theologico-Politicus* (1670), and by John Locke in his *Two Treatises of Government* (1690). Both Spinoza and Locke had also anticipated Rousseau's ideas on religious toleration and on the "reasonableness" of religion. The enormous popularity of Rousseau's work was due not to its novelty, but to the fact that it was expressed in popular language and came at a time when the whole continent felt that the absolutist system had outlived its usefulness. The middle classes of Europe had grown wealthy and influential over more than a hundred years of relative peace. Conscious of their power, they resented the privileges of the two first estates, the clergy and the nobility, which, in spite of warning voices within their own ranks, forced the government to employ unjust measures of taxation, jurisdiction, and administration. In addition, the peasantry was cruelly exploited. Rousseau showed the dissatisfied what nature demanded not only in education but also in politics. And, of course, they listened. Even today, Rousseau is regarded as a prophet by the struggling intellectuals of Asia, Africa, and South America.

JOHANN HEINRICH PESTALOZZI

Pestalozzi had many things in common with Rousseau. Although he was a theist and a sincere believer in the gospel of Christ, he shared Rousseau's alienation from the life and teaching of the established churches. He, too, had an aphoristic mind, was loath to undertake the systematic pursuit of an academic discipline (which probably preserved his creativity), was subject to depressive moods, and was unable to live and work with other people. Both suffered all their lives from the feeling that their love for mankind remained unanswered. Even in the heat of their work they were unable to extricate themselves from their tense and ever-questioning self.

Yet, whereas Rousseau was apparently incapable of real devotion and sacrifice, Pestalozzi was possessed of the power of altruistic love, the deep desire to help men not only through ideas but through sharing their lot in the concreteness of actual situations. As a person, Rousseau was attracted by the privileged; Pestalozzi, by the poor.

In 1779, about a century and a half after Comenius wrote his

Great Didactic, and seventeen years after the appearance of Rousseau's *Émile,* Pestalozzi, in a night of desperate search for clarity
about himself and his work, jotted down a series of loosely connected aphorisms, *The Evening Hours of a Hermit (Die Abend-
stunde eines Einsiedlers).* This work is regarded by some as the most
profound brief essay ever written about the education of man.
The Evening Hours begins with the following words:

> Man who is the same whether in the palace or in a hut, what is he
> in his innermost nature? Why do not the wise tell us? Why are the
> greatest of our thinkers not concerned with knowing what their race is?
> Does a peasant use his ox without knowing it? Does not a shepherd
> care for the nature of his sheep?
> And you who use man and profess that you guard and nurture him,
> do you care for him as the peasant cares for his ox? . . .
> What man is, what his needs are, what elevates and humiliates him,
> what strengthens and what weakens him ought to be the most impor-
> tant knowledge for the rulers as well as for the humblest.[9]

Out of this theme Pestalozzi develops his ideas about the nature
and the maturing of man, or, to use modern terminology, his
philosophical anthropology. Central for him is the idea of suc-
cessively widening circles of experience, each of which must be
fully mastered before a person can enter the next. The infant
must feel embedded in the love of the mother before he can join
the family. The child must feel the protection of the home before
he can become a member of the community. Only with the help
of cooperating communities can a nation be built; and only those
who are at home in their country can understand mankind. Whoever is insecure in the smaller will be still more insecure in the
wider circle. He will never find "his truth." Truth, here, denotes
not an intellectual proposition that gives a person the feeling of
correspondence with a reality *outside* himself; rather, it means the
person's sense of correspondence *within* himself. It is the same as
"being true to oneself," or authenticity. Only from this kind of
authenticity will come maturity and happiness—the only happiness
man can achieve.

Hence there cannot be the same education for everybody. Those
who confuse the equality of man before God and the law, or the
dignity and the natural rights of man with equality in intellectual

---

9. For a partial translation of Pestalozzi's *The Evening Hours of a Hermit* see
R. Ulich, *Three Thousand Years of Educational Wisdom, op. cit.,* pp. 480–85.

achievement, knowledge, and status, will only help in the process of social disintegration and self-alienation, which, as Pestalozzi realizes, are the great dangers at a time when youth is taught to accept symbols that have no meaning, to use words that carry no responsibility, and to develop ambitions that are beyond reach.

One could call *The Evening Hours of a Hermit* a psychological essay written by an eighteenth-century existentialist. Indeed, there is an existentialist flavor in Pestalozzi's whole work and personality. But one would have to add immediately that his was not the existentialism of a Heidegger or a Sartre, but that of a Kierkegaard or a Gabriel Marcel. For, after discussing the psychological and social conditions of a person's way toward self-identity, Pestalozzi passes from the existentialist level of the human career to the metaphysical level. All human relations, he asserts abruptly, can fulfill their ethical purpose only when they receive their strength and inspiration from the center of all creation, which is God. This conviction of the inseparability of human productivity from its divine source remained with Pestalozzi throughout his life. It was this conviction which, in all likelihood, saved him from transgressing the borderline between extreme sensitiveness, with all its creative qualities, and psychopathic affliction. Sometimes he was near to the latter.

All the later works of Pestalozzi could be described as an unfolding of the leitmotiv already given in *The Evening Hours. Leonard and Gertrude (Lienhard und Gertrud, ein Buch für das Volk,* 1781–85), the work that made him famous, illustrates Pestalozzi's conception of creative living and education within a specific social situation. A morally and economically decaying village is rescued when the patriarchally minded lord of the land discovers that salvation can come only from the grass roots. In the school he intends to found, he will follow the principles that Gertrude, the wife of a poor mason, applies in the upbringing of her children.

In no way does Pestalozzi disregard the value of established institutions. Though a revolutionary in his student years, he has now become socially conservative. He accepts the authority of the landlord, and he demands strict discipline and the teaching of religion. But all this is of no avail, he insists, unless teachers understand how the "ways of nature" operate as a person learns and matures. Thus Comenius' idea of method as the discovery of the inner laws of life recurs in Pestalozzi's concept of organic or elemental education, though it is now cleared of the pseudoscientific encumbrances that mar the ideas of the seventeenth-century theologian.

Only once did Pestalozzi try to analyze his educational ideas according to psychological categories. That he calls the resulting work *How Gertrude Teaches Her Children* is, in a way, misleading, for the great merit of the mason's wife is that she has no psychological theory but uses a mother's intuition, educated and formed by love, the Bible, and bitter experience. Pestalozzi himself is aware that "the mechanism of physical human nature" from which he wants to derive the right methods of instruction is not really a mechanism but an organically structured whole. Consequently, when he bases the child's learning on the three basic elements of "sound, form, and number," he conceives of the various mental capacities as functioning within a creative totality. Pestalozzi's work simplifies the complicated process of cognition. However, with the recent emphasis on "structure" in learning [10] we may read his reflections in a new spirit of appreciation.

Inevitably, Pestalozzi, with his intense interest in the development of the person within society, was attracted and at the same time repelled by the trends of his time. He was attracted by the progressive ideas of the Age of Enlightenment and by the original motives of the French Revolution—the insistence on liberty, fraternity, and equality. He shared in the opposition to oppressive and exploitative feudal institutions, and he sympathized with the fight against unjust governments allied with an insensitive and reactionary clergy. Moreover, he shared the conviction that only a total reform could save Europe from decay.

He was repelled by the intellectualism of the principal representatives of the Enlightenment, the French *philosophes,* and by the satirical vein in which they criticized the Christian religion, confusing its institutions with its essence. He abhorred the remoteness of so many enlightened men from the real life of the people and the gap between their gospel of social and moral reform and their personal conduct. He was onesided in this respect, especially after the defeat of his hopes in the French Revolution, which first had made him one of its honorary citizens. He deplored the devas-

---

10. See J. S. Bruner, *The Process of Education,* Cambridge, Mass.: Harvard Univ. Press, 1960.

tation that the French armies brought to his own and other countries. Also, he was disappointed in Napoleon.

Thus he abandoned his early enthusiasm for Rousseau and no longer dared hope for the universal progress that he and the rationalists of the eighteenth century had envisaged. In his profound essay, *My Inquiries into the Course of Nature in the Development of Mankind (Meine Nachforschungen über den Gang der Natur in der Entwicklung des Menschengeschlechts,* 1797), he concluded that progress appears only in the achievements of rare personalities, not in the behavior of people in general.

Perhaps he would have looked differently at the world if the various schools he had founded, first at Neuhof, then at Stans, Burgdorf, Münchenbuchsee, and, finally, Yverdun, had given him the feeling of success and lasting satisfaction. That this was not the case was partly his own fault. His psychological constitution made him a bad administrator. He did not know how to select the teachers he needed, and he spoiled even the devotion of those who would have followed a steadfast guide. Yet it was through the combination of writing and practical school work that Pestalozzi attracted the attention of European and American leaders in thought and education. What these men saw at Pestalozzi's schools was a program of studies that brought the younger generation closer to the life around them, that replaced drill with observation and motivation, that respected the individuality of the pupils, and that replaced the sense of fear and punishment with a sense of mutual cooperation.

Despite the earlier work of the then largely forgotten Comenius, all this was rare at the time of Pestalozzi. That which in his day was still an experiment is now required of the schools to which we entrust our children.

FRIEDRICH FROEBEL

When we consider the line of educational development from Comenius to Rousseau and Pestalozzi, it is difficult not to think at the same time of the German Friedrich Froebel. He also endeavored to implant as it were, the mental life of the growing person in the creative ground of nature, or, in other words, to save the natural initiative of the child as he is taught to participate in the complicated enterprise of human culture.

One of Froebel's inspirations came from a visit he paid in 1805 to Pestalozzi's school at Yverdun. This visit would have taught him little if he had not already felt the urge to improve the conditions of mankind as a teacher of the young, and if, moreover, he had not been influenced by the romanticist conviction of the essential identity between the life of man and the ever-evolving cosmos. The thinker who in Froebel's time most impressively expounded the idea of the essential unity between mind and nature was the philosopher Friedrich Schelling. Indeed, if one were looking for a philosophical systematization of the ideas consciously and unconsciously underlying the educational thought of Comenius, Rousseau, Pestalozzi, and Froebel, one would find it in Schelling's "transcendental philosophy."

Compared with his predecessors Froebel knew more about nature in the scientific sense of the word. Before becoming an educator, he had been apprenticed to a forester and had studied science at the University of Jena. Nevertheless, his main pedagogical work, *The Education of Man (Die Menschenerziehung)*, as well as his autobiography, reveals the romantic more than the scientist. "My religious life"—he says in his autobiography—"now changed to a religious communion with nature." Nature was for him neither an inanimate order nor merely the great sustainer, but the great teacher. His autobiography contains an exquisite passage in which he tells us about the scruples Froebel had about the mysteries of procreation.

> But my eldest brother, who, like all my elder brothers, lived away from home, came to stay with us for a time; and one day, when I expressed my delight at seeing the purple threads of the hazel buds, he made me aware of a similar sexual difference in plants. Now was my spirit at rest. I recognized that what had so weighed upon me was an institution spread over all nature, to which even the silent, beautiful race of flowers was submitted. From that time humanity and nature, the life of the soul and the life of the flower, were closely knit together in my mind; and I can still see my hazel buds, like angels, opening for me the great God's temple of Nature.[11]

The work that shows him not only as one of the great educators, but also as one of the great philosophical minds of the nineteenth century—provided one does not exclude from philosophy the great

---

11. F. W. A. Froebel, *Autobiography,* tr. by E. M. and H. K. Moore, London: Allen & Unwin, 1886, p. 12.

intuitions as to the role of man within the greater universe—is his *Education of Man.* At the beginning of this book Froebel attempts a kind of ontology of education by advancing the idea that humanity, when engaged in the process of education, represents the highest stage of cosmic development. Evolution, which is for Froebel a gigantic process of inner-directed activity, goes on in progressive stages of consciousness, from inanimate nature through the animal kingdom to the kingdom of man, where the instinctive impulse is joined and elevated by the human being's awareness of his participation in the cosmic energy.

> In all things there lives and reigns an eternal law. To him whose mind, through disposition and faith, is filled, penetrated, and quickened with the necessity that this cannot possibly be otherwise, as well as to him whose clear, calm mental vision beholds the inner and the outer and through the outer, and sees the outer proceeding with logical necessity from the essence of the inner, this law has been and is enounced with equal clearness and distinctness in nature (the external), in the spirit (the internal), and in life which unites the two. This all-controlling law is necessarily based on an all-pervading, energetic, living, self-conscious, and hence eternal Unity. . . . This Unity is God.[12]

These words indicate the principles underlying the practice of Froebel's educational work. There can be no real education that is not self-education or self-activity, for the universe of which we are a part dooms to decay all that ceases, or is not motivated, to shape its course in harmony with the process of creation. Because this process is continuous, all learning must also be continuous. There is a passage in *The Education of Man* that might almost have appeared in one of Pestalozzi's writings:

> How different could this [human development] be in every respect, if parents were to view and treat the child with reference to all stages of development and age, without breaks and omissions; if, particularly, they were to consider the fact that the vigorous and complete development and cultivation of each successive stage depends on the vigorous, complete and characteristic development of each and all preceding stages of life! [13]

Naturally, these principles affect Froebel's conception of the curriculum. Unless subjects are taught as interacting rather than sep-

---

12. F. W. A. Froebel, *The Education of Man*, tr. by W. N. Hailmann, New York: Appleton, 1892, p. 1.
13. *Ibid.*, p. 28.

arate units, the information received will have no really formative
effect on the maturing person. The result may even be confusion.
Furthermore, even in early childhood the program of studies should
be arranged in such a way that it reflects the totality of the world
to which the young are to be introduced. It should contain religion,
not as a fixed set of dogmata, but as a dynamic mental enterprise.
"Religion is not something fixed, but an ever-progressing and, for
this very reason, ever-present tendency." [14] The second subject
should be nature. "What religion says and expresses, nature says
and represents. What the contemplation of God teaches, nature
confirms." The third subject is language. "Language represents the
unity of all diversity, the inner loving connection of all things."
Finally, there is art. It is connected with all the other areas of the
curriculum—religion, nature, and language. Yet it can also be a
pursuit of its own when cultivated as the representation of man's
inner life, differentiated in accordance with the material it uses.

> A universal and comprehensive plan of human education must, there-
> fore, necessarily consider at an early period singing, drawing, painting,
> and modeling; it will not leave them to an arbitrary, frivolous whim-
> sicalness, but treat them as serious objects of the school.

The importance that Froebel attributed to play as the early expression of the inner activity of man is well known and has decisively influenced our understanding of early childhood.

In our age of sober technicality it is difficult to read Froebel
without a feeling that one is being confronted with sentimentality.
Yet he was a manly man who valiantly participated in the German
war of liberation against Napoleon, only to hear in 1851, the year
before his death, that the Prussian government had banned the
already-flowering kindergarten movement. In addition to his liberalism, his pantheistic conception of religion was certainly one of
the reasons for the ban. In Prussia's insane rage against all that
seemed to be related to the Revolution of 1848, Froebel's nephew
was sentenced to death, though he was pardoned and later honored
after the unification of Germany in 1871. Nor could Froebel's work
be suppressed for long. After ten years the kindergarten movement
developed with new vigor, so much so that public opinion connects him almost exclusively with the education of the very young,

---

14. This and the following quotations are from Froebel's *The Education of Man,*
   ibid., pp. 140, 151, 209, and 228.

though much of his wisdom applies also to later stages of human development.

SUMMARY

Comenius, Rousseau, Pestalozzi, and Froebel were men of different ages, different character, and different backgrounds. Yet there are many reasons for grouping them together. They all searched for a method based on psychological understanding of the child's learning instead of subjecting the child to goals and ideals set by adults without regard for his aptitudes.

It is, of course, a fallacy to believe that the immature child can determine the aims of his education, which would mean the aims of the culture into which he is beginning to grow. But it makes a great difference whether this process of "growing toward" is imposed upon him from outside, or whether it is directed with a minimum of pain and a maximum of motivation and participation. If the latter is achieved, we may expect a sound and productive adult instead of a resentful and twisted personality.

This is what Comenius and his successors meant when they spoke of happiness and freedom, of organic education, and of self-activity. They believed they had found the key to the new method in nature. The cultural contingency and the vagueness of the concept of nature are obvious. Although the concept arose from a strong inner experience, it was more an evangel than a logical and empirical proposition.

Paradoxically, the conviction of the evangelists was reinforced by a seemingly contradictory trend, the confidence in the new method of the empirical sciences. For instead of evoking a cool sense of accurate and relativistic research, these sciences were welcomed as the harbingers of a new era in which the world of nature and the world of man would no longer be divided but would harmonize with each other.

This hope was understandable. To the contemporaries of Galileo and Newton it meant escape from a world of magic, religious fanaticism, and superstitious fears into a world of tolerance, understanding, order, and a degree of predictability. Moreover, men felt that the admirable results of the new scientific method proved the validity of the concept of natural law. This concept, originally Stoic, had always been based on the conviction that there is an inner unity among the laws of God, nature, and man. When these laws were applied to the political situation, they vindicated the opposition of liberal minds to the unnaturalness of the political and religious absolutism of the time.

Indeed, at the time of Rousseau and Pestalozzi the culture of the comfortable classes had reached such a degree of artificiality that the new and protesting generation spoke the word "nature" with a religious fervor. Before the French Revolution even the courtiers and their wives and mistresses read idyllic poetry and played shepherd in the parks on their estates.

Taking all these trends together, one can understand the sense of mission among the progressive educators of the time. They were the great enthusiasts in the history of Western education. In fact, there were many more of them than the few great leaders mentioned here. In eighteenth-century Germany, for example, men like Johann Bernhard Basedow, Christian Gotthilf Salzmann, and Joachim Heinrich Campe, generally called the representatives of "philanthropinism," began to influence the school system through their insistence on natural methods of teaching.

The educators discussed in this chapter would not have achieved what they did had they not been inspired by a genuine sense of love for the young and growing. From Comenius to Froebel we discover an increasing appreciation of the sanctity of childhood. The helplessness, playfulness, groping, and romping vitality of the child were, according to them, not merely something to be corrected or a sign of "original sin," but an indication of the self-evolving unity of nature and mind within a dynamic universe. Granted that an overdose of this sentiment might turn into sentimentality, still, the absence of it is considered by cultured people as evidence of an insensitive mind.

Suggestions for Class Discussion and Further Investigation

1. What was the influence of the Reformation on education? If you had been a teacher at the time of the Reformation, how might your work and your career have been affected?
2. Why is this chapter entitled "The Seventeenth Century: Education for Communion"?
3. How might American education have been altered if Comenius had accepted an invitation to become the first president

of Harvard College? How did Comenius' views on education differ from those of the men who set the pattern for higher education in America?

4. Why is the *Great Didactic* called a milestone in the history of education?
5. How can you account for the divergence of opinions about the work of Rousseau?
6. To what extent are Rousseau's views of education applicable to American schools today?
7. What similarities—and what differences—do you find between Rousseau and Pestalozzi? Which of the two held views of the natural state of man that are most nearly consistent with those of twentieth-century anthropologists?
8. Comenius, Rousseau, Pestalozzi, and Froebel—all searched for ways of understanding the child and the learning process. How did their conclusions differ?

Chapter Six

The Age of Reason:
Education for Independent Thinking

THE BACKGROUND

The phase of education to which we now turn coincides largely, though not perfectly, with the Age of Reason or the Enlightenment.[1]

The men who molded the mentality of this period shared many ideas with the enthusiasts described in the last chapter. Never were the so-called rationalists merely cool and calculating intellectuals, as they often have been characterized, or men with no sense of the transcendent qualities that bind human beings to one another and to the universe. They too were capable of great passion. Denis Diderot, who as the editor of the *Encyclopédie* (*Encyclopédie, ou Dictionnaire raisonné des sciences, des arts et des métiers*) became one of the most influential apostles of the rational spirit, began his *Philosophical Contemplations* (*Pensées philosophiques*), one of the best sources for an understanding of the Enlightenment, with the following words:

> One constantly argues against the passions. One blames them for all the afflictions of man. But one forgets that they are also the sources of all his happiness. Passion is, in man's constitution, an element to which one can attribute neither too much good nor too much evil. However, that which irritates me is the fact that one sees in passions only their bad qualities. One believes it is doing an injustice to reason if one speaks in favor of its rivals. However, it is only the passions, and the great passions in particular, which inspire the soul with a sense of greatness. Without them, nothing sublime, in morality as well as in action! The arts would return to infancy, and virtue would become pedantic. . . .

1. For a general interpretation of this period see E. Cassirer, *The Philosophy of the Enlightenment*, tr. by F. C. A. Koelln and J. P. Pettegrove, Princeton: Princeton Univ. Press, 1951, and A. Cobban, *In Search of Humanity: The Role of the Enlightenment in Modern History*, New York: Braziller, 1960.

One should then—so you will tell me—congratulate a man for his strong passions. Certainly, but only, if they work in unison. Establish the right harmony among them, and you will not need be afraid of confusion. If hope is balanced by prudence, sense of honor by love for life, the penchant for pleasure by care for health, then you will have no libertines, no foolhardy people, and no cowards.[2]

This is good Aristotelian ethics but in no way a recommendation of abstinence from the risk of a fully lived life. Even Rousseau could not have objected to it.

Like Comenius and his followers, the rationalists based their hopes for the progress of mankind on the advance of science and on a methodical approach to the problems of nature and humanity. The verbal kinship between Comenius' concept of light and the term "Enlightenment" reveals a deep unity of meaning. Like light or understanding for Comenius, reason for the rationalists was not just an isolated faculty but a power interwoven into the whole making of the world. And however much the rationalists were influenced by Newton (almost all of them were believers in the supreme value of mathematics), they too, with the exception of a few materialists, believed in nature and natural law not merely as a causal nexus but as the ultimate source of form and creation and hence as the criterion of right thinking and conduct.

Beginning with the Frenchman Pierre Bayle, whose *Dictionnaire historique et critique* (a forerunner of Diderot's *Encyclopédie*) prepared the way for the skeptical and analytical attitudes of the eighteenth century, many of the *philosophes* sacrificed their personal welfare for the victory of the ideas of freedom and toleration. In this respect too they resembled Comenius and his successors. Many of them came from the nobility, and all of them could have had comfortable lives instead of lives of danger and persecution had they not set principle above convention.

Even with regard to religion one has to avoid the familiar generalization that the whole Age of Reason was hostile to faith as an element in the human search for meaning. In no other century have educated laymen argued more about religion than in the eighteenth. Their debate, however, was no longer on the level of that of the Reformation and Counter Reformation, when but a few (quickly eliminated) heretics dared doubt the truth of the Christian gospel. Rather they debated, psychologically, in a

---

2. D. Diderot, *Œuvres complètes*, Paris, 1818, vol. 1, pp. 105 *ff.*

mood of profound disappointment with the endless quarrels over dogmatic subtleties that had lost their original meaning, and, intellectually, on a level of cognition raised above that of earlier times by the scientists before and after Newton.

There can be no doubt that in France, Voltaire's famous dictum *"écrasez l'infame"* (crush the infamous), by which he himself meant the corrupt ecclesiasticism of his time but not religion as such, engendered a wholesale and one-sided attack on Christianity by certain contributors to the *Encyclopédie,* such as Holbach and La Mettrie, and, to a degree, Diderot himself. Religion came to be regarded as a force invented by cunning rulers to prevent man from using his reason for a better, freer, and more dignified life. At the height of the French Revolution, in 1791, Volney, author of *The Ruins, or Thoughts on the Revolutions of Empires (Les Ruines, ou Méditations sur les révolutions des empires),* anticipated Marx's characterization of religion as an opiate for the people.

In England the critical theory of knowledge, expounded by David Hume in *An Enquiry Concerning Understanding* and his *Dialogues on Natural Religion,* increased distrust of the validity of all a priori assumptions, theistic as well as deistic, a distrust which the empiricism of John Locke had already foreshadowed. But Locke left the core of religious faith untouched by his critical analysis of knowledge, which, if pursued radically, should have ended in agnosticism. Rather, he made himself believe that he had proved philosophically the necessity for a "natural" religion and the existence of God. He even made his own personal Bible from Holy Script. The ax of Hume's logic went much deeper; it cut into the roots.

Yet the prudence of the English, including that of a good part of the Anglican clergy, led them to follow Locke rather than Hume, while large segments of the English middle classes and, especially, the working people remained firmly in the Biblical tradition, as a result of the missionary work of pious sectarians, among them John Wesley. It is to the credit of the workers that, despite all the exploitation they suffered during early industrialism, they did not turn Marxist and atheistic, as did many workers on the Continent.

The effect of the Enlightenment, or the *Aufklärung,* as the Germans call it, was even less disruptive in Germany than it was in England. One reason is that the division into two major denominations, the multitude of states, and the absence of an intellectual center such as Paris prevented a nationwide alliance of the liberal forces against the elements of retardation. To be sure, the German absolutist princes also put their opponents into prison. As late as 1732 Bishop Firmian of Salzburg could dare to force 22,000 Protestants out of his territory. On the Protestant side, the orthodox clergy could no longer expel heretics. And yet, as they had persecuted the mystic Jakob Böhme for his theosophical speculations at the beginning of the seventeenth century, so in the eighteenth they persecuted the poet and philosopher Lessing and other free minds for their enlightened and tolerant ideas.

However, there prevailed among the educated the moderate deism of the philosopher Christian von Wolff, who tried to reconcile reason and revelation, faith and evidence. Not until the rise of the philosophical systems of Kant, Fichte, Schelling, and Hegel, and the ascent of the new and scholarly type of university, was Germany to assume a leading role, and for some decades *the* leading role, in thought and research. Kant insisted on the distinction between valid criteria of intellectual truth on the one hand and intuitive and subjective certainties of faith on the other. Inevitably, this insistence, coupled with his criticism of the traditional proofs of God and his rationalist writings on religion, aroused the opposition of the clergy and the government, which anyhow suspected him of being sympathetic to the French Revolution.

Yet, instead of being called "the great destroyer," as he was by his opponents, he should have been called "the great bridge-builder," for he established a synthesis between Descartes' over-optimistic belief in the universality of reason and Hume's radical skepticism. Moreover, in his moral philosophy he admitted that there exists one instrument—moral conscience—by which man's mind can reach into the absolute.

Fichte, accused of atheism and forced to renounce his chair at the University of Jena, tried to reconcile the monistic determinism of Spinoza with the human postulate of free will. Hegel's philosophy of self-unfolding reason as the driving force in history was the most comprehensive systematization of the faith of the seventeenth and eighteenth centuries in the central role of reason in man's destiny. Finally, when Schelling developed a system in which he tried to explain the absolute as an integration of nature and mind, he confirmed philosophically the idea of the communion between man, nature, and God that had inspired the great educators before his time.

All these idealistic systems provided a sense of continuity between the older and the newer forms of thought. After their appearance one could no longer be satisfied with the intuitive visions of Comenius or with an insufficiently examined rationalism. However, the proponents of these systems advocated a world view in which the intellect should understand itself only as one of the media available to man in his unending search for the meaning of life. Vision and creative intuition were also expressions of reason.

Viewing the Age of Reason as a whole, we cannot deny that in spite of all its exaggerations and mistakes (and what productive period is free of them?) it was a period of liberation. Specifically, it freed humanity from the burden of dynastic and clerical privilege, from witch trials and torture, from the imprisonment of thought, from the handling of women and children as property—taken altogether, from the imposition of obsolete traditions on the progressive elements of society. Today some philosophers and theologians with existentialist leanings criticize the Age of Reason as the beginning of the "self-alienation of modern man" and other spiritual evils. One can only reply that these very critics might have been burned or exiled if the rationalists had not taken up the fight for freedom of expression we now enjoy, at least in some countries. The task has not yet been completed; perhaps it is beyond the boundaries of human achievement. Today, we are in some respects farther away from the ideals of the eighteenth century than many of us believe. All the greater is the obligation to have our minds open to the greatness and courage of the Age of Reason.

EDUCATION

The French Revolution. One of the accusations frequently leveled against rationalism is that it was responsible for the French Revolution and its excesses. Yet, considering the social injustices in absolutist France this revolution would have occurred even if there had been no *philosophes.* Had the Enlightenment not provided an ideological basis, the disappointed people might have appealed to the Christian Gospel, as did the rebellious poor in the Middle Ages and the Renaissance, and some of the pre-Marxian socialists in the nineteenth century.

From the point of view of the historian of education, dissatisfaction with political and religious absolutism and the desire for a more rational and national form of education had set in in France even before the revolution. Louis René de Caradeuc de la Chalotais, an aristocrat in high office, demanded in his *Essay on National Education* (*Essai d'éducation nationale*, 1763) that the obsolete Jesuit colleges be replaced by modern institutions under national auspices. Even Catholic monarchies resented the clerical influence on national affairs. In 1773, Pope Clement XIV yielded to the governments of Portugal, Spain, and France and suppressed the Jesuit order, which in those countries had dominated the secondary schools and universities. However, the French Revolution exceeded expectations by eliminating all ecclesiastical influence from the schools and by making the priests appointees of the state.[3] It tried to establish a secular, pragmatic, and specialized education by means of *Écoles Centrales,* which were a mixture of secondary and higher schooling, and of *Écoles Spéciales,* which were separate professional institutions designed to replace the hated universities. But in spite of glowing accounts of future projects, written by men like Turgot, Diderot, Talleyrand, and Condorcet, and in spite of the laws governing elementary and secondary education issued under Robespierre in 1794, the reforms were either not put into practice or else failed.

Nevertheless, failure in the beginning does not always mean failure at the end. The French Revolution made the governments of Europe aware that people were not merely material objects and reminded them that the populace might revolt and even decapitate a king—as the English had learned in 1649. To use Jefferson's phrase, Europe realized "that the mass of mankind has not been born with saddles on their backs, nor a favored few booted and spurred, ready to ride them legitimately, by the grace of God." [4]

One had seen what could happen when fanatical leaders became the slaves of an uneducated mob. Universal elementary education, which had already been initiated on the European continent by the German states, was gradually understood—last of all in England —to be not only a boon to the poor but a benefit to the nation as

---

3. The *Constitution civile du clergé*, 1790.
4. T. Jefferson, "To Roger C. Weightman, June 24, 1826," in *The Writings,* ed. by A. A. Lipscomb, Washington, D.C., 1903–04, Bk. XVI, p. 182.

a whole, especially since the intricacies of politics, technical production, warfare, and communication demanded a literate citizenry.

Some Forerunners of Rationalist Education. If we are to trace the impact of the rationalist spirit on educational thought, we must not restrict ourselves to the usually accepted chronology which connects that spirit too narrowly with the eighteenth century. However rare critical reason may be, it is nevertheless an old and enduring trait in human culture. Signs of a rationalist protest against the religious tradition had appeared in the Middle Ages.[5] Humanist critiques and satires preceded Voltaire. Not only Erasmus, Von Hutten, and Brant, whom we have already mentioned, but Rabelais —in *Gargantua* and *Pantagruel*—used the weapon of irony against monkish education. Montaigne, author of immortal essays, addressed a letter to a French noblewoman in which he wrote the following words:

> I would have the tutor make the child examine and thoroughly sift all things and harbour nothing in his head by mere authority or upon trust. Aristotle's principles should no more be axioms to him than those of the Stoics or Epicureans. Let different judgments be submitted to him; he may be able to distinguish truth from falsehood; if not, he may remain in doubt.[6]

John Locke, one of the first great figures of the Enlightenment, was greatly indebted to Montaigne in his essay *Some Thoughts Concerning Education,* in which he put the importance of a sense of reality, wise management of one's affairs, and an intelligent character far above traditional book learning.[7] Although Locke was writing after the time of the English "commonwealth educators," [8] who during the period of the Republic, from 1649 to 1660, had outlined a scheme of practical education for the rising middle classes, he revealed no sympathy for the masses. His writings, like those of Montaigne, and Chesterfield's *Letters to His Son,* seem to regard wise and tolerant reasoning as the privilege of the gentleman. Nor was Voltaire any more interested in having his ideas disseminated

5. See. R. Ulich, *The Education of Nations,* Cambridge, Mass.: Harvard Univ. Press, 1961, pp. 7 *ff.*
6. M. Montaigne, *The Education of Children,* tr. by L. E. Rector, New York: Appleton, 1899, p. 31.
7. J. Locke, *Some Thoughts Concerning Education,* ed. by R. H. Quick, London: Macmillan, 1902.
8. See R. Ulich, *History of Educational Thought, op. cit.,* pp. 178 *ff.*

among the masses. From his point of view, they needed a solid dose of Christian supernaturalism to remain content with their lot.

The Absolutist Princes. As a matter of fact, some of the Catholic charitable orders and some of the absolutist princes of Germany,[9] cared more for the welfare and education of the poor than did the philosophers. It is misleading to call these princes despots, for this term connotes tyrant. Some of them behaved despotically, but others, sometimes even the same ones—think of Czar Peter I (the Great) of Russia—had a genuine interest in the welfare of their people. Especially in the German realm they demanded compulsory school attendance, often against the resistance of the privileged classes and the people.

The Archduchess Maria Theresa of Austria, an absolutist ruler, issued in 1774 the *General Law for the Schools of Austria,* which was anything but despotic. It begins with the words:

> Having nothing more at heart than the true welfare of the countries which God has confided to us, and having always attentively considered whatever might contribute to this end, we have observed that the education of both sexes, the basis of the real happiness of nations, requires our special care. This very important object has the more attracted our attention, inasmuch as the future destiny of man, the genius and thought of entire nations, depend mainly on the good instruction and right training of children from their tenderest years. Such an object, however, can never be attained if the darkness of ignorance is not dispelled by well regulated instruction and education, so that every individual can acquire knowledge according to his ability and condition.[10]

After his final victory over Austria, Frederick the Great of Prussia, a deist and the host of Voltaire (but also the host of the Jesuits when both were exiled from France), promulgated in 1763 his *General Regulations of Elementary Schools and Teachers,* which begin as follows:

> Whereas, to our great displeasure, we have perceived that schools and the instruction of youth in the country have come to be greatly neglected, and that, by the inexperience of many sacristans (*custos*) and

---

9. For the development of public education in Germany during the seventeenth and eighteenth centuries see K. A. Schmid, *Geschichte der Erziehung,* Stuttgart, 1896, vol. 4, Part I.

10. See E. P. Cubberley, *Readings in the History of Education,* Boston: Houghton Mifflin, 1920, p. 474.

schoolmasters, the young people grow up in stupidity and ignorance, it is our well considered and serious pleasure, that instruction in the country, throughout all our provinces, should be placed on a better footing, and be better organized than heretofore. For, as we earnestly strive for the true welfare of our country, and of all classes of people; now that quiet and general peace have been restored, we find it necessary and wholesome to have a good foundation laid in the schools by a rational and Christian education of the young for the fear of God, and other useful ends.[11]

Nevertheless, all these regulations, most of which were issued in the seventeenth and eighteenth centuries, breathed the spirit of "our paternal care for the welfare of our faithful subjects." [12] With large parts of the rural population still semiliterate or without any schooling at all, this was probably the best that could be hoped for. But it was an offense to the city population, which during the eighteenth century reached a level of economic and cultural wealth often superior to that of the ruling classes.

Nevertheless, under German enlightened absolutism an academically respectable science of education (*Wissenschaft der Pädagogik*) began to influence the quality of elementary and secondary schools. These schools absorbed more and more of the rationalist spirit that had entered the professions after the founding of the progressive universities of Halle (1694) and Göttingen (1734). Soon other countries looked to Germany as the main source of educational theory and practice.

German Idealism. Finally, during the decades around 1800, the German idealistic philosophers wrote a number of profound treatises on the nature, education, and destiny of mankind. Even Kant found time to give a course on this subject. It is preserved only in posthumously edited notes made by his students, and these notes give us an incomplete picture. Nevertheless, his listeners must have felt that they were in the presence of a great man when they heard him say:

> There are many germs, lying undeveloped in man. It is for us to make these germs grow, by *developing his natural gifts* in their due proportion, and to see that he fulfils his destiny. . . .
> Education is an *art* which can only become perfect through the prac-

---

11. *Ibid.*, p. 459.
12. Frederick the Great, "Silesian School Code of 1765," in Cubberley, *ibid.*, pp. 466 *ff.*

tice of many generations. Each generation, provided with the knowledge of the foregoing one, is able more and more to bring about an education which shall develop man's natural gifts in their due proportion and in relation to their end, and thus advance the whole human race toward its destiny. . . .

One *principle of education* which those men especially who form educational schemes should keep before their eyes is this—children ought to be educated, not for the present, but for a possibly improved condition of man in the future; that is, in a manner which is adapted to the *idea of humanity* as a whole and the whole destiny of man. This principle is of great importance. Parents usually educate their children merely in such a manner that, however bad the world may be, they may adapt themselves to its present conditions. But they ought to give them an education so much better than this, that a better condition of things may thereby be brought about in the future.[13]

No wonder, then, that the professors of the University of Königsberg welcomed, as Kant's successor, a scholar who was not only sympathetic to the master's critical philosophy but who was also interested in education. That scholar was Johann Friedrich Herbart. Herbart had visited Pestalozzi at Yverdun and had reviewed some of his work. But while he shared the enthusiasm of his time for the mission of education in the life of humanity, he also knew that its success depended on a thorough understanding of the processes involved in knowing, learning, and teaching. Thus he became the great pioneer of an exact psychology of education to whom all later leaders are indebted. Even Sigmund Freud acknowledged that he had learned from Herbart.

The significance of Herbart's work lies in his methodical observations of the ebb and flow of mental experiences, which he called "presentations." These observations caused him to reject the old theory of the existence of separate mental faculties, such as intelligence, feeling, and will. The so-called faculties, he thought, must be understood as reactions of the whole mind and the whole person to changing environmental stimuli, which, of course, evoke at one time one, and at another time another, form of self-consciousness. Sometimes a rational, sometimes an emotional, and sometimes a volitional response will come to the fore in order to preserve the person in his unique and indestructible individuality. According to Herbart, the human mind works like an inner

---

13. The notes have been published in I. Kant, *Education,* tr. by A. Churton, Ann Arbor: Univ. of Mich. Press, 1960. See pp. 9 *ff.* and 14.

mechanism (an unfortunate term, though it had already been used by Pestalozzi). Certain ideas, or presentations, tend to dominate the mental scene for a while. But as new experiences arise, those presentations are pressed under the threshold of consciousness, or, as we say, they are forgotten. Under the impact of new stimuli they may emerge again, or be remembered. Forgetting, therefore, is not a negative, but a productive, part of the economy of the mind. When properly appealed to, seemingly forgotten experiences will reappear, relate themselves to new presentations, and thus provide the continuum that a human being needs for survival.

It is, therefore, the task of the teacher to motivate the pupil in such a way that every new presentation offered in the course of instruction arouses the perhaps sleeping, but still existing, deposit of memories, or, as Herbart called it, the "apperceptive mass" behind and within the stream of consciousness. The effective teacher discovers which new presentations appeal to the child's interest and understanding, motivates his sense of participation, and thus helps him to overcome the difficulties that are inevitable if the child is to adapt himself successfully to the intellectual standards of our complex civilization.

Therefore, a good school will see to it that the program of studies is not a medley of incoherent facts, but a continuum. While the good teacher respects the objective requirements of civilization without any sentimentality, he pays attention also to the individuality of the learner.

In order to achieve this goal the teacher will do well to proceed in four steps. First, he will make clear what he intends to teach. Second, he will associate the new knowledge with that already acquired by the student. Third, he will show the student that the new knowledge stands within a logical structure and belongs to a larger, comprehensible context. And fourth, he will awaken in the pupil a desire for a methodical rather than a haphazard approach to knowledge. These are Herbart's famous "four steps" (preparation, presentation, association, and systematization), to which the Herbartians later added a fifth step, "application." In a deep sense, the five steps are the transfer of Pestalozzi's idea of organic circles of experience from the general human to the intellectual level of learning. But while Pestalozzi grasped the truth intuitively, Herbart, the scholar, grasped it analytically.

Nothing has done more harm to the reputation of a great mind such as Herbart's than the pedantic teaching of the four (or five steps in institutions for the training of teachers, although Herbart himself warned against applying them mechanically. Nevertheless, even the most experimental and imaginative methods of instruction are harmful only if they neglect the principles that Herbart laid down and tried out in his own university seminar for prospective teachers. If the so-called progressive movement in the United States had understood how to build enough Herbartian wisdom into its own theory and practice, we would have had a steady instead of an unsteady transition from the old to the new.

As a philosopher Herbart was too empirical and critical to admire unconditionally the flights of *Weltanschauung* performed by the idealist-romantic philosophers. Remaining close to Kant, he opposed the confusion of poetry and philosophy he believed he found in them. Herbart—who shared with almost all the great philosophers, from Pythagoras and Plato, an exalted opinion of mathematics—regarded philosophy as a science whose task is:

> . . . to procure a consistent organization and procedure within the multitude of general ideas! It should bring about an interconnection among the fundamental concepts of all the various fields of scholarship. Thus it should help the individual person to gain a comprehensive view of human knowledge and, moreover, to integrate his own thoughts and raise them to a higher level of efficiency.[14]

For Herbart this clarifying and uniting task of philosophy was unthinkable without a metaphysics. In the formation of that metaphysics he was more aware of the scholar's obligation to look for verifiable data than were his famous contemporaries. Yet his attempts to bring about a unity between metaphysics and science were not free from obscurities and contradictions. This explains why the Herbartian educators, impatient with his involved thinking, separated the master's psychology and theory of education, which they rightly considered useful, from its philosophical background, which they considered unnecessary. But when an intellectual whole is divided into parts there is always a danger that the parts will lose their content. This is exactly what happened with the psychology and the pedagogy of the Herbartians. They lost Herbart's concept of the soul as a dynamic and self-preserving

---

14. J. F. Herbart, *Lehrbuch zur Einleitung in die Philosophie*, in *Sämtliche Werke*, ed. by G. Hartenstein, Leipzig: Meiner, 1850, vol. 1, p. 33, par. 3.

entity—a concept that had brought him close to Leibniz's theory about monads and Aristotle's theory about entelechy, conceived of as forces striving to maintain themselves within a constantly changing and struggling world. They gave their teachers only prescriptions for methods of teaching, useful for the average (who are always in the majority) but stifling to those endowed with imagination and enthusiasm.

Whatever our opinions about Herbart's whole philosophy, no one can deny the merits of his attempt to place the newly emerging science of pedagogy into the totality of scholarly pursuits. His comprehensive view helped him to appreciate the intuitive insights of the enthusiasts from Comenius to Froebel, as well as the logical ambitions of the rationalists from Descartes to Hume and Kant. He provided for his time an educational synthesis that was important both for the systematic preparation of teachers and for the organization of public instruction. There is no one, perhaps with the exception of Pestalozzi, to whom our schools are more indebted than to Herbart.

His role in the history of thought would be insufficiently described if it were related only to education. The empirical part of his system gave the scientists of the nineteenth century a welcome philosophical basis for their protest against the dominance of the schools of romantic idealism.

While Hegelianism declined, in education and elsewhere, Herbartianism rose. The book *Pedagogics as a System (Die Pädagogik als System,* 1848), by Karl Rosenkranz, who applied Hegelian dialectics rigidly to educational problems, was ridiculed by the Hebartians. Strangely enough, only in the United States did it enjoy a prolonged reputation. Translated into English in the 1870's, it was highly esteemed by the Hegelians in St. Louis, Missouri. Nevertheless, the metaphysical faith of their leader, William T. Harris, did not prevent him from reforming the curriculum of the St. Louis schools by emphasizing the role of science, the arts, and practical subjects. He soon attracted national attention and became in 1889 the U.S. Commissioner of Education. During the seventeen years of Harris' tenure the influence of Hegel was on the wane. In 1892 the National Herbartian Society was founded, and its members had a decisive influence in the remodeling of American instruction according to more modern psychological concepts. They were supported by Commissioner Harris, who, wisely enough, chose to emphasize the similarities rather than the differences between the two German philosophers.

In our discussion of Herbart it may seem as though we have been dealing with an educator who had little to do with the rationalist movement, which is the main subject of this chapter. Chronologically, we certainly have gone beyond the period of Diderot, Hume, and Kant. Yet, seen from a wider perspective, Herbart as an educator belongs to the rationalists. For him religion played a minor role in the formation of character, though he declared that his metaphysics postulates the idea of immortality.[15] Though he was deeply interested in esthetics, being himself an accomplished musician, the mystical experiences characteristic of many artists were alien to him. He could find words of intuitive depth, but his whole style of thinking and writing was that of a primarily logical mind. It was his unrelenting logic that paved the way for the discovery of the subconscious and with it a new theory of man, a new philosophical anthropology. Thus, while his theory of the learning process was in one sense a fulfillment of the past, it pointed at the same time toward new depths of thought.

Suggestions for Class Discussion and Further Investigation

1. The Age of Reason has been described as a period of liberation. From what were people being liberated?
2. How did this liberation affect the goals of education and the content of curricula?
3. Contrast the influence of German rationalism on education with that of English empiricism.
4. How did the French Revolution affect education?
5. What were Napoleon's views on the proper responsibility of the schools?
6. Locke's ideas about the learning process have often been misinterpreted by educators. After reading his essay, *Some Thoughts Concerning Education,* what do you consider the proper application to education of his *tabula rasa* principle?
7. In what different ways did the ideals of the Enlightenment affect education in England, in France, and in Germany?

---

15. *Ibid.,* vol. 1, p. 267, par. 153.

Chapter Seven

The Effect of the Rationalist
Attitude on the American Concept
of a Free and Pluralistic Society

THE FOUNDERS

It was in North America that the rationalist spirit achieved its
political and educational fulfillment. Unlike Europe the new continent had never been buried under a load of feudal traditions.
The Puritan orthodoxy of New England maintained its regime
only up to about 1700. Even before that time, Roger Williams,
author of the *Bloudy Tenent of Persecution for the Cause of Conscience* (1644) and founder of Rhode Island, had already protested
against the persecution of people because of their religious convic-
tions. The early settlers were men and women with a spirit of
adventure, and many of them had suffered political and religious
persecution at home. Though most of them were of English or
German origin, they soon realized that the country could be developed only by people willing to live together under a variety of
ethnic and religious conditions. Furthermore, the American Revolution, unlike the French Revolution, was not a revolt of hungry
masses led by inexperienced theoreticians, but a war of liberation
and a process of reorganization guided by men whose courage and
enthusiasm were checked by reason and prudence.

Thus, the conditions were present under which the ideals of the
Enlightenment could ripen: recognition of the natural rights of
man, social and legal justice, the separation of political power from
religious institutions, constitutional guarantees, the absence of
despotism, and the participation of the people in the affairs of the
state—in brief, all that we now comprehend in the term democracy.

Of course, this development did not occur without resistance.
In certain respects, especially with regard to the racial problem,

the United States is still far from achieving these ideals. Old traditions asserted themselves also in education, for immigrant groups, in order to preserve their cultural identity within a foreign environment, often stick more obstinately to the past than do people in their home country. This helps explain the emphasis on classical learning at Harvard College from its very beginning to the nineteenth century. When Yale in 1827 sensed the wind of innovation, it advocated the preservation of the old liberal arts with a conviction that could not have been surpassed by Oxford or Paris.[1] Even the "Report of the Commission of Ten on Secondary Studies" of 1893 shows a certain predominance of the ancient languages over the more modern studies, though that predominance was already waning.

To be sure, a preference for the classics is quite compatible with a rationalist and progressive spirit. For many centuries this spirit had drawn its nourishment from Greek and Roman literature. The scholasticism of Thomas Aquinas, which was a form of progressive rationalism within the Christian heritage, throve on the logic of Aristotle. Plato was the source of inspiration for the members of the Academy of Lorenzo Medici. The oratory of the French Revolution was spiced with quotations from the ancient, for the Athenian and Roman republics were regarded as the great patterns of a free commonwealth. And the classics were admired by two men who symbolize the rise of the American democratic and rational spirit more than anyone else: Benjamin Franklin and Thomas Jefferson. Franklin was the ideal representative of the rising middle class, with its moral code of order, industry, and thrift added to the more lofty virtues of the Greco-Christian tradition. Jefferson was the very picture of the aristocrat who regarded the advantages of his birth not as a prerogative but as an obligation. Generosity and a sense of the beautiful were as natural to him as if he had inhaled them from infancy. In contrast and as his autobiography shows, Franklin, the son of a craftsman, had to acquire his stature through learning and self-discipline.

There is no need to describe in detail Franklin's attempt to establish a school system that, notwithstanding the values of a liberal education, was to serve the industrial and mercantile classes. In his

---

1. See R. Ulich, "The American University and Changing Philosophies of Education," in *Issues in University Education*, ed. by C. Frankel, New York: Harper, 1959, pp. 29 *ff*.

pamphlet *Proposals Relating to the Education of Youth in Pensilvania* (1749) he recommended an "Academy" which besides a classical department should harbor an "English School," divided into a department of modern languages (French, German, and Spanish) and a department of mathematics and "natural and mechanic philosophy" for students interested in experimentation and observation.

The growth of the English School was prevented by prosperous Philadelphians who sought to acquire prestige for themselves and their children by emulating the traditional education of the upper classes. (The ambition of parents to achieve status through the education of their children, even though the children may not profit from it, is still a widespread social phenomenon.) Some decades later, Franklin's proposals for a practical as well as a liberal education led to the institution of "Academies" for students with nonacademic aspirations. In the second half of the nineteenth century, however, with the spread of the public high school, most of these academies lost their purpose. In a kind of reverse trend, those that survived became boarding schools with a selective liberal arts program.

Nor is there much need to emphasize Thomas Jefferson's political and educational ideas, which were based on a rationalist interpretation of the natural rights of men. These ideas motivated him to fight "the impious presumption of legislators and rulers, civil as well as ecclesiastical, who, being themselves but fallible and uninspired men, have assumed dominion over the faith of others." [2]

However, Jefferson's emphasis on the equality of all men and on their right to be educated [3] never led him to confuse equality of opportunity with equality of achievement. Rather, like Franklin he demanded that the broad educational base and the rise of general knowledge which a republic should provide be combined with a selective process and the promotion of superior quality. Therefore, he devoted the last years of his life to the development of the University of Virginia, which he had founded and for which

---

2. Act for Establishing Religious Freedom, passed by the Virginia Assembly on the Revision of the Constitution, 1776.
3. Bill for the More General Diffusion of Knowledge, presented to the Virginia Legislature, 1779.

he—being an architect of high rank—had laid out the building plan. As a result of his leadership the new university was for some time the most modern institution of higher education in the United States, and, together with some German universities of the time, the freest in the world.

The pragmatic idealism of such men as Franklin and Jefferson has become a part of the American tradition and still has great appeal to Americans. Should it disappear, the United States would be a very different country.

JOHN DEWEY AND PROGRESSIVE EDUCATION

The convergence of rationalism, pragmatism, and idealism in the national climate of the United States explains why, a hundred years after Franklin and Jefferson, John Dewey became the leading American philosopher and the spiritual guide of the nation's teachers. Unfortunately, many of those teachers never read his books thoroughly, contenting themselves with an occasional quotation.

Dewey tried to integrate his thought with social and intellectual developments that could not have been foreseen by the men of the eighteenth century. He combined Hegelian intuitional evolutionism with scientific and social Darwinism. He was concerned with modern technology and its effects on a largely urbanized population, so different from the population of Jefferson's time. His life coincided with the rise of trade unions and with the development of Marxist socialism in Europe. After having preached the gospel of democracy with the inner certainty of a prophet, he observed the growth of totalitarianism and communism and the changes in the constellation of the world powers. Finally, as an educator he tried to assess the effect of all this on a population of one hundred and fifty million, largely immigrants, whose children were attending high schools as well as grade schools.

Despite the differences in the historical situation, we can sense in Dewey's work the spirit of Franklin and Jefferson as believers in the rights and potentialities of the common man, but Dewey's debt to Herbart has not been sufficiently recognized. His work *How We Think* (1909) is in essence a Herbartian treatise. Only by referring to the deplorable loss of historical tradition among American teachers can we explain why they considered Dewey's work an entirely new approach to education. He himself never denied his indebtedness to the past. In his essay "From Absolutism to Experimentalism" he declared that Hegel and Plato had "left a definite deposit" [4] in his thinking. In his essay "Evolution and Ethics" he expressed the hope that there is an interaction between our ethical laws and "the working processes of the universe," and that man "in this moral struggle . . . acts not as a mere individual but as an organ in maintaining and carrying forward the universal process." [5] A religious element can be found also in Dewey's *My Pedagogic Creed* (1897), though the primary emphasis of this work is social. When the teacher—Dewey says—becomes aware of the dignity of his calling and helps to "secure social growth," then he "always is the prophet of the true God and the usherer in of the true kingdom of God." [6]

But this was the early Dewey. His main work was marked by the dilemma of his strong idealistic leanings and a fear that his "philosophy of experimentalism" might be weakened by the assumption of metaphysical apriorities and "fixed aims." He never made it sufficiently clear to his followers that experimenting, in science as well as in education, needs a purpose in order to be truly experimental, and that all the great aims mankind has pursued in the course of history, such as freedom, love, and justice, were not "fixed" or "absolute," but directed toward ever-receding horizons, and also experimental in a sense.

Dewey's haziness in regard to the nature of aims was especially evident in his treatment of the problems of ethics and their application to education, as one can easily gather from a critical reading of his famous work *Democracy and Education* (1916), especially the eighteenth chapter on "Educational Values."

PROGRESSIVE EDUCATION

Dewey's name has been connected with a once much-praised, and now much-criticized, American movement called progressive educa-

4. G. P. Adams and W. P. Montague, eds., *Contemporary American Philosophy*, New York: Russell and Russell, 1963.
5. J. Dewey, "From Absolutism to Experimentalism," in *The Monist*, 8 (1898), pp. 321–41.
6. J. Dewey, *My Pedagogic Creed*, reprinted in R. Ulich, *Three Thousand Years of Educational Wisdom, op. cit.* There is also an extract from "Evolution and Ethics."

tion.[7] Partly rightly and partly wrongly, this movement has been accused of encouraging subjectivity without a complementing sense for the objective duties of man, of exaggerating the principles of activity, motivation, and child-centeredness, and of neglecting coherence and discipline in instruction as a result of its obsession with the experimental spirit. For all these defects John Dewey has been held responsible.

Although Dewey cannot be absolved from all responsibility, in his (much too benevolent) *Experience and Education* (1938) he pointed out the dangers of undirected experimenting. So did some of his outstanding disciples. But the damage was done, partly because the early warnings of such wise men as W. C. Bagley, H. H. Horne, and I. L. Kandel had gone unheeded.

It did much harm to Dewey and the progressive movement that teachers of the highest quality had to work along with dilettantes whose enthusiasm for change remained untouched by even the slightest knowledge of the enduring elements in education. These dilettantes represented the historically well-known type of disciple who is the greatest enemy of his prophet. They demanded that students be critical, but were themselves unable to discover the weaknesses in the master's thought, especially his dangerous identification of statements of aims and of idealistic and religious philosophies with "absolutism" and "authoritarianism." They decried conservatism in education and politics as a vice but proved that shouting for change and progress does not protect a man against dogmatism in his own mind.

Now, when it has become fashionable to blame Dewey and progressive education for everything that was wrong, let us restore some balance. Only ignorant or reactionary men can deny the merits of the progressive movement, wherever it has appeared. At a time when in this country, more than in any other nation with an advanced school system, many teachers went into their classrooms with a textbook from which they slavishly read to their bored pupils, and when in other countries educators were still submitting to reactionary authorities and relieving themselves of their inferiority feelings by beating their pupils, men and women with a professional conscience felt bound to look for reform. Among these

---

7. See L. A. Cremin, *The Transformation of the School: Progressivism in American Education, 1876–1957*, New York: Knopf, 1961.

men and women were *Les Compagnons* in France, the members of
the New Education fellowship which started in England, and the
Resolute School Reformers in Germany. The latter group was influenced partly by Marx, but partly also by Pestalozzi, and was
unhappily divided by the conflicting influences. Shocked by the
debacle of the First World War, they all desired an education that
would help young people use their learning for critical participation in the affairs and responsibilities of modern society. The coming generations—these progressives thought—should not be molded
by teachers who themselves had been molded by obsolete conventions and national and religious ideologies. Instead of answering
questions that their students had never asked, teachers from the
elementary schools to the universities should encourage young
people to find their way into and through a society afflicted by uncertainty and conflict. Though the goal might be utopian, the spear
of hope must always be aimed farther than it will fall. The teachers who started these progressive movements were not the mediocre
ones; in Europe they often came from highly idealistic youth movements. The mediocre ones were on the other side.

Now one may ask: What have all the progressive dreams accomplished? After the First World War—the Second World War!
Here I may be permitted to refer to a personal experience. During
the rise of National Socialism a number of university professors
(some of whom were not even German) recommended to me Hitler's
Mein Kampf as a book of extraordinary quality. Certainly the quality is extraordinary—not high, as they thought, but incredibly low.
All these professors had gone through demanding formal schools.
Many of them had read Plato in the original, and probably all had
studied Cicero as the great master of style and the defender of
justice. So, being myself an admirer of classical studies, I often ask
myself: "What have *they* accomplished?" Apparently, in the period
of the world wars (are we out of it yet?) there were forces at work
against which not only teachers but even statesmen of good will
were helpless. If these sinister forces are to be warded off, then
let us hope that a truly progressive and courageous spirit will
remain among teachers, though few will deplore the demise of
American progressivism as an organization. We must at the same
time hope that these teachers will be able to work and strive within
a framework of thought mature and complete enough to combine a

desire for improvement with a sense of the permanent values in human culture.

Suggestions for Class Discussion and Further Investigation

1. What is meant when the United States is referred to as a pluralistic society?
2. How did Benjamin Franklin's idea of education differ from that of most educators of his time? How do you account for the difference?
3. How did Jefferson's views on education differ from Franklin's? On what issues did the two men agree?
4. If Jefferson were alive today, what would be his reaction to the argument that all high-school graduates should be admitted to college?
5. John Dewey has been called "the father of progressive education." Is this an accurate or a misleading statement of his true relationship to the progressive movement?
6. Write a short paragraph summarizing as accurately as you can Dewey's educational philosophy. Why is Dewey's philosophy more difficult to state clearly than that of some other educational philosophers?
7. In what respects did Dewey's philosophy differ from that of the leaders of progressive education in the 1930's?
8. As viewed from the perspective of today, what appears to have been the long-range influence of the progressive education movement?

Chapter Eight

Education for Information

In our description of the philosophical dilemma of Dewey and the progressive movements, we have already suggested the state of bewilderment that is characteristic of our time. To be sure, earlier periods, too, experienced confusion. Crises impel people to raise questions, to act, and to reorganize their affairs. In that sense, crises are a requisite of progress. But our time surpasses the earlier ones in that the foundations of man's self-consciousness, conscience, and confidence have been shaken by a cruel contrast: an overwhelming increase of scientific and historical knowledge on the one hand, and, on the other, a volcanic eruption of the brutality in man, with the suicide of humanity now being more than an apocalyptic dream.

The turning point in Western civilization was the First World War, when, according to an English statesman, the lamps went out all over Europe. Then, in 1918, there appeared such books as Oswald Spengler's *Decline of the West* (*Der Untergang des Abendlandes*). This book, first rejected by a number of publishers, would not have had the amazing international success it did had it not struck a chord in the hearts of thinking people all over the world. As a matter of fact, the first crevices in the cultural tradition of Europe had already opened in the decades before Spengler. The Frenchman Auguste Comte had declared in his *Positive Philosophy* (*Cours de philosophie positive,* 1830–42) that the theological stage of history (representing man's childhood) and the metaphysical stage (representing the adolescent's desire for speculation) should be replaced by a positivistic or scientific stage of mental maturity.

From England came Darwin's theory of evolution and the moderate but stirring positivist philosophy of Herbert Spencer. The shift in the professional preparation of these thinkers is noteworthy. Whereas the idealistic philosophers came from classical and partly from theological schools, Comte received his academic training at the famous École Polytechnique of Paris, and Spencer had studied engineering and economics.

The classicists, too, rebelled. Marx had received his doctorate in

philosophy with a thesis on Greek philosophy, *The Difference
Between the Natural Philosophies of Democratus and the Epi-
cureans,* before he wrote the *Communist Manifesto* in 1847 and
Capital in 1867. In the latter work he promulgated the theory that,
not Hegel's "World Mind," but the forces of production determine
the political, social, and educational conditions of a given society.
Everybody was eager, to use a Marxian term, "to turn Hegel upside
down." Also in Germany there appeared the most radical critic of
Christianity, Friedrich Nietzsche, whose power over the minds of
youth was enhanced by the fascination of his style.

All these men were critics of the existing school system, especially the secondary and higher schools, though for different reasons. Darwin, in the *Autobiography* and in a July, 1853 letter to
W. D. Fox, objected to "the enormous proportion of time spent
over the classics." Spencer, in *Education: Intellectual, Moral, Physical* (1861), compared the cultivation of the classical languages with
tattooing used as a means of social distinction by primitive tribes.
Nietzsche, himself for some time a professor of the classical languages, declared in his various comments on the future of education that pedantic teachers could not convey the value of antiquity
to students ignorant of the beauty and literature of their mother
tongue.

At the same time religious instruction, which was obligatory in
European schools, had become conventional, often given by teachers so impressed by modern science and Biblical criticism that they
could not accept the tenets of the denominational catechisms that
they were forced to teach. For reasons partly political and partly
religious, France finally achieved the separation of State and Church
in 1905, leaving the nation dangerously divided between liberals
and conservatives. Inevitably the churches moved from passive
resistance to aggressive action. Countries with a predominantly
secular school system saw the rise of denominational institutions.
On the Catholic side they were powerfully supported by the encyclical of Pope Pius XI on "The Christian Education of Youth"
(1929)[1] which declared it the duty of all Catholic parents to keep
their children away from schools whose curricula were not per-
meated by a Catholic interpretation of life. Before Pius XI, Pope

1. Pope Pius XI, *The Christian Education of Youth* [*Divini illius magistri*],
New York: America Press, 1936.

Leo XIII had already issued the famous encyclical on "The Condition of Labor" (1891),[2] which had had a twofold effect: politically,
it had acknowledged the right of labor to organize; religiously and
educationally, it had made Catholic workmen more self-conscious
and had thus prevented them from identifying themselves with the
socialist labor unions and their secular ideology.

Besides the universities believing in the Spinozistic idea of *libertas philosophandi,* there have arisen higher Catholic schools which,
however, differ greatly with regard to denominational strictness.
In France, Belgium, and the United States, many of their teachers
are not even Catholics, while others are unwilling, or not even
required, to submit their work to ecclesiastical control. Science,
especially, proves to be impervious to the influence of religious
creed. Moreover, books on evolution like those of the Catholic
cleric and scientist Pierre Teilhard de Chardin, as well as books on
existentialist philosophy, are gaining increasing attention among
Catholics.

Nevertheless, the Catholic schools, especially in the lower grades,
still have a center of concentration and, consequently, a measure of
discernment as to what should be taught first and last. In contrast,
the secular schools are wide open to the influx of new subjects, each
of which may be somehow desirable, but which in their accumulation disorganize the unity of the curriculum and endanger the inner order that is necessary for the steady progress of learning as well
as for intellectual and ethical maturity. Unfortunately, the easiest
and therefore the most popular subjects are favored by many
communities.

The venerable three R's, which in earlier times determined the
teaching of the elementary schools, are now surrounded and pene-
trated by civics, biological exercises, and introduction to the visual
arts—all desirable, but truly effective only when they are properly
integrated with the basic objectives of elementary learning. On the
whole, grade schools have been enriched by a more creative approach to the child's learning. In contrast, secondary schools all over
the world are in a state of confusion, intellectually as well as
institutionally.

The traditional classical-humanist ideal has lost its hold over
the minds of youth. There was a period of revival during the

---

2. Pope Leo XIII, *Encyclical Letter: On the Condition of Labor,* Boston, 1891.

decades before and after 1800, when great classical scholars opened
new vistas for the understanding of the Greek and Roman cultures.
Creatively fused with the ideas of romanticism, immersion in the
spirit of the ancients was considered a means of regaining a stronger
sense for the depth of man and his tradition, now threatened by
the superficialities of a decaying rationalism and the dangers of
rising industrialism.

In Germany the flowering of ancient studies was fostered by the
enthusiasm of Goethe, Hölderlin, and other poets for the charm
and wisdom of the Greeks (often unrealistically interpreted as
the symbols of human perfection). France, believing itself the true
heir of Roman greatness, considered the study of its language a
matter of national pride. In England the famous Public Schools
saw in classical literature the best means of deepening the meaning of the gentleman ideal, which had become a matter of empty
convention.[3]

In spite of its irreplaceable value, the classical ideal, mainly historical in character, was contingent upon a cultural configuration
largely dominated by the old-type scholar and the clergy. With the
rise of new scientific and technical occupations it became identi-
fied with backwardness—unfortunately, not without some justifi-
cation. Like all "neo" movements the neo-humanism of the nineteenth century indicated a tendency to escape the challenge of the
present. Soon it lost the breath of vitality.

But the struggle over the value of the classics, though still continuing, is but a minor part of the new trends in education. Not
only the secondary schools, but education in all its manifestations,
have during the twentieth century been deeply affected by a new
interpretation of learning—the emphasis on the developmental
phases of cognition and comprehension.

One of the most manysided scholars of modern times, Wilhelm
Wundt, physician, physiologist, psychologist, philosopher, and an-
thropologist, established in 1879 at the University of Leipzig a
laboratory where he advanced the efforts of his predecessor, Gustav
Theodor Fechner—and, in a way, also those of Herbart—to explain
psychic phenomena in relation to physiological processes.

Among the many disciples who came to Leipzig from all parts of

---

3. On the gentleman ideal see R. Ulich, *The Education of Nations, op. cit.,*
pp. 97 *ff.*

the world was the American G. Stanley Hall, who made Clark
University the center of developmental psychology at a time when
William James of Harvard was carrying on his psychological experiments, preparing his famous *Talks to Teachers on Psychology and
to Students on Some of Life's Ideals* (1899), and writing his still
more famous lectures, in *Pragmatism.* The developmental psychology of Stanley Hall permitted the teacher to understand better the
various stages in the growth of the individual from infancy to
maturity, while William James' functional psychology gave them
a deeper insight into the interaction of body and mind, conceived
of as the individual's instruments in his struggle for survival. Both
psychologists had an overwhelming influence on the theory and
practice of American education, and when their disciple, Edward
Lee Thorndike, devoted his long and rich career at Teachers
College, Columbia University, mainly to the psychology of education, the United States became the leader in these areas. Alfred
Binet of the University of Paris and Louis William Stern of the
University of Hamburg were prominent figures outside America.

The importance of psychometry was enhanced by the two World
Wars when the selection and classification of men for specialized
tasks became a matter of survival, but even more so by the necessity
of mastering the gigantic influx into our schools of pupils with
diverse talents. Today, industry, hospitals, and hundreds of public
and private agencies could not work without psychometric labora-
tories.

In spite of its merits, the testing movement met with opposition
among the liberal-arts departments of universities all over the
world. Critics suspected that because of its quantitative orientation
it might bring a materialistic, if not vulgar, aspect into the sacred
halls of learning. Indeed, its experiments concerning the interrela-
tion of various psychic activities and the effect of the learning of
certain subjects on general mental progress (so-called transfer) were
detrimental to old and cherished prejudices about the unique value
of primarily verbal studies, which so far had enjoyed high prestige
in erudite circles. As many roads lead to Rome, so there were, in
the opinion of the new experimenters, also many ways of becoming an intelligent, inventive, and generally cultured person.

In itself testing as a science can never claim to offer any final
judgment on the value of a special study. Nor did any one of the
pioneers in the field do so. Herbart, as we know, was a metaphysi-

cian; Fechner was a mystic; one of the many works of Wundt was on ethics; Hall was a theologian as much as a scientist; and if we want to go back far enough in history, we would have to mention the Spanish Catholic Huarte de San Juan of the sixteenth century as one of the first who tried to relate psychological to physiological processes, in his book *Examen de Ingenios para las Ciencias* (1575, translated in 1594 by Richard Carew as *The Examination of Men's Wits*).

Yet it cannot be denied that many of the new specialists, swimming self-assuredly on the swelling wave of testing, were unwilling (or unable?) to ask themselves to what extent quantitive data could be applied to qualitative mental phenomena. In their understandable enthusiasm for the results of statistics they made an idol of the intelligence quotient and the shaky results of their transfer experiments. Animal psychology—a most worthwhile study if properly interpreted—seemed to them more enlightening than what the philosophical, religious, and artistic traditions had to say about humanity. Thus they trespassed their boundaries and had, for a while, an antihumanistic influence on American schools.

With a certain historical logic the testing movement in the United States coincided with the flowering of pragmatism, also called experimentalism. The pragmatic emphasis on "process" and on "learning by doing" directed the attention of educators one-sidedly to the problem of methods and led confused minds to the conclusion that almost everything was worth teaching, provided there was somebody to teach it to somebody willing to learn. Thus, concern for the immediate, often even for the trivial, endangered the reasons for the long-range cultural purposes of education.

This development was supported by the rising influence of new social classes that had little understanding for the older and sometimes hypocritical criteria of good breeding, gentility, and a universal liberal education, but which emphasized instead the value of "usefulness." Under their pressure the curriculum-makers failed to see that there is rarely a criterion that lends itself to so many false interpretations as does utility. Added to it were such emphases as the "independent value of childhood," "need-satisfaction," and "life-adjustment."

All these pedagogical concepts have their place in education. Who ever wants the useless, or, still worse, who ever wants to be useless? Even the medieval universities, so often praised for their devotion to the sublime, prepared young men for the professions. And the so-called disinterested studies of the gentleman had, and still have, their practical value. Nobody wants to have maladjusted children. Just as in our times we have too many Philistines, so in earlier times there were too many snobs who lived egotistically on inherited money.

The ultimate criterion, in education as elsewhere, is whether a nation produces a sufficient number of people with a sense of responsibility and right proportion. This sense is impossible without an inner center from which one can see things in proper perspective or the one within the whole to which it belongs. There is no historical proof that in earlier times there was more of this rare quality than there is now, but we may need it more than our ancestors did.

Naturally, the cultural and social changes in the environment have affected not only the curriculum but the structure of the secondary schools. They, like the universities, have become less exclusive. Whereas in the Europe of 1900 only about 3 per cent of the school population between the ages of 10 and 19 attended schools that allowed their graduates to go on to a university, the percentage has now risen to about 25. While the European countries (which do not have the unique American institution of the four-year college between high school and graduate school) have been slow in expanding their universities, in the United States over 1,900 institutions offer some kind of instruction beyond the secondary level to about 39 per cent of young men and women.

In conservative Europe the division between the academic secondary schools (Public Schools and Grammar Schools in England, *Lycées* and Colleges in France, *Gymnasia* in Germany, *Ginnasi* and *Licei* in Italy) and the nonacademic schools has been maintained, but the injustices of the old bifurcation have been lessened by a number of measures that facilitate transfer from one to the other form of schooling.

It is easy to imagine the effect of all these innovations on the program of studies, on the maintaining of standards with regard to both teachers and pupils, and on the role of education in the life of modern nations. Furthermore, responsibilities unforeseen two generations ago have been imposed on our schools by rapid and continuing changes in industrial production with the concomitant loss of individual apprenticeship, by the change from rural to urban life, by the increase of leisure time, by automation, and last, but not least, by the change in the role of the family. Many a family is today nothing but a functional instrument to provide for the survival of its members for as long as they need it. This explains, on the one hand, the growth of kindergarten and pre-kindergarten institutions and, on the other hand, the increase in juvenile delinquency—many of the delinquents merely stranded adventurers who in earlier times would have gone to work on a farm or a ship.

Under the weight of these changes the schools find it difficult to chart their course. They would find it so even if our civilization were still held together by some transcendent faith. But must such a faith by necessity be of supernatural character in the older sense of the term, a belief in God, in Christianity, or in some other revealed religion?

Many believe so. They tell us that the misery of our time stems from unbelief, or from the errors of humanism, naturalism, and other "atheistic cults." Certainly, some of the greatest cultural advances have come from theistic, or at least metaphysical, inspirations. But others have come from other sources, often against the opposition of the defenders of traditional piety. Also, the question must be raised why in earlier times, which are supposed to have been more religious, men cared apparently less for the common welfare than they do today in civilized nations.

As to the controversy between "naturalism" and "supernaturalism" (whatever the terms may mean) the historian is confronted with questions he cannot answer for lack of evidence. Unfortunately the philosophers will not help him because, since the time of Socrates and the Sophists, they have disagreed on the nature and origin of morality.

Yet, despite the hopeless battle of opinions, the problem of values is crucially real for the educator, for he is constantly called upon to make decisions. Up to the eighteenth century all education was under sectarian control. Today the religious issue appears in the educational policy of all Western nations, with the United States and France on the secular side. But, as their parliamentary debates, legal decisions, and, especially, administrative practices prove, they too are involved in compromise and contradiction. England, in the meantime, is happily "muddling along" in a form of mitigated conservatism, and several states of the German Republic demand that instruction be based on Christian principles, although there, as in other countries, many teachers are agnostics at heart. Only the communist countries are outspokenly anti-religious.

The worldwide conflict will engulf the new nations as well. So great is the confusion that we do not even know which side represents the old viewpoint and which represents the modern, for new developments in religion, orthodox as well as unorthodox, claim to represent the modern mind more clearly than the older Comtian or Spencerian positivism.

Under these circumstances many teachers, from the elementary school to the university, withdraw from the conflict of theories and decide "to stick to their subject matter," honestly believing, or making themselves believe, that their students will not discover their bias. The result is a skeptical, if not cynical, mood among the most sensitive members of the younger generation, especially in Germany and in other countries which during the past decades have undergone ideological extremes. Conscientious teachers observe this development with anxiety and would like to help their pupils but, conscious of the surveillance of religious or political groups, they do not want to risk their jobs and the security of their families. Along with the sociologists, they observe that young people do not care for politics. From what source are they to acquire that interest? To whom will politics be left if young people in our advanced schools do not want to become involved? It is a sign of decay that in the United States the word "politician" has become a derogatory term. In England it is not.

Education, then, in contrast to all that has been demanded by the great teachers of mankind and by the much-blamed progressive movements, becomes a matter of mere training, schooling, and information-gathering. Without bothering about the deeper problems of human existence, the "curriculum makers" can wrangle over the number of hours that should be allotted to foreign languages, science, social studies, sports, and driver education. With the intellectual and spiritual burden of the past too heavy, conflicting opinions too many, school hours and corrections and useless paperwork too time-consuming, and school administrators too anxious for peace—what else can remain but the teaching of skills and subject matter?

This, of course, is a pessimistic outlook that, to a degree, we will correct later. There is not, however, sufficient comfort in the continual quantitative increase of our secondary-school curriculum or even in the laudable attempts of good teachers to "keep up to date" with the constantly swelling subject matter. For, on the not-yet-specialized level of pre-university teaching, this is well-nigh impossible. Even specialists in our graduate schools can no longer read all the published articles that relate to their interests.

Still less should we comfort ourselves with the idea that we will be able to delegate part of the drudgery of schooling to teaching-machines and other mechanical devices. Certainly, anything that allows the teacher and the pupil more time to discuss the principles by which knowledge is acquired should be welcomed without prejudice, but always in full awareness of the fact that the machine may become the master of the man instead of the man remaining the master of the machine. While no one will deny the real and potential blessings of television, we are all concerned about the losses it has inflicted on self-activity, on the inner life of the family, and on the sense of quality.

Frightened by the remarkable achievements of Russian science and technology—though not from this motive alone—we have now replaced the former emphasis on the average learner (sometimes called "the cult of mediocrity") with the postulate of excellence. The "common man" is for a while out of fashion, though he will remain the solid earth in the garden of civilization. But excellence can be more than high-grade specialization only when it is achieved by a whole and morally healthy person. "To strive for excellence and surpass all others" was the battle cry of the Homeric heroes. They were certainly no models of civilized conduct. All depends on where and for what purpose we want to surpass others. If, rightly impressed by Soviet efficiency, we ourselves make mere efficiency the main goal of our education, we may suddenly discover that we have lost the best of it in the process.

Suggestions for Class Discussion and Further Investigation

1. Why is this chapter titled "Education for Information"?
2. Spengler, Comte, Darwin, Spencer, and Marx were all critical of the schools they saw around them, but for different reasons. What were some of the reasons of each?
3. What were some of the ways in which the psychologists of the

late nineteenth and early twentieth centuries—Wundt, Hall, James, and Thorndike, for example—influenced education?

4. What have been the influences of the testing movement on education?

5. What is the meaning of the word "experimentalism" as applied to education? How is experimentalism related to pragmatic philosophy?

6. Progressive views of education were less influential in parochial schools than in either public or independent schools? Why? Is the situation changing today?

7. Examine the meaning and implications of the phrases, "cult of mediocrity," "excellence," and "common man."

8. How does the Catholic view of education differ from that of most Protestants? Why are Catholics more eager than most Protestants to send their children to parochial schools?

Chapter Nine

Education for the State

We would have an incomplete picture of Western education without some discussion of the role of the State in the life of the schools, for no major activity in a modern society can escape its influence. It affects our vocations and professions, our economic and physical welfare, and our systems of communications from highways to newspapers. Through public taxes we support our research, our defense, even our art. How could education remain free?

The absolutist states that arose during the fifteenth and sixteenth centuries formed the first big corporations with a permanent bureaucratic staff. The philosopher Thomas Hobbes wrote of the new "Leviathan." The bureaucracy has been given more and more power, partly because we hopefully believe that we control it by our parliaments. But to what degree does it rule over us? Rousseau had no illusions when he declared that the English nation—at his time the exemplar of a constitutional state—had a voice only during elections. Only in the Swiss cantons, he thought, was the government truly in the hands of the people.

The concern of the State with education has varied in the course of time. In prepolitical tribal societies education was integrated into the total life of the group. It molded the individual member more effectively than in our own complex environment with its many loopholes for the eluder. Primitive man knew that the mistake of one might be detrimental to the whole. Hence, he gave a ritualistic character to the upbringing of the young, for men believed that deities and ancestors were easily offended and might refuse to protect the tribe if the elders failed to initiate their sons and daughters into the sacred customs. One has but to read the first verses of the *Odyssey* to learn of the intimate connection between the inhabitants of Olympus and the fortunes of mortals. And however much Plato was embarrassed by the primitiveness of Homeric theology, his own writings, the *Republic* and the *Laws*, still reflected the intrinsic unity of education, worship, and the

State. Despite our admiration for the genius of Greece, we have
to admit that the city-states, in their constant fear of one another,
were not yet far above the tribal situation.

But a disturbing question emerges. We no longer live in small
states made up of from 10,000 to 100,000 inhabitants. But we have
spies everywhere; we spend our resources and our manpower for
armament; and we envy the scientific progress of other countries
instead of enjoying it as a contribution to knowledge. We still fight
wars as cruel as were those between Athens, Sparta, Corinth, and
Thebes, but on a scale a thousand times larger. And never has
indoctrination for chauvinism been so skillfully used as in our
times.

The modern state has used three methods to influence the
schools. These methods have sometimes crossed, and the nomen-
clature we will use to explain them is as defective as are all
classifications of complex human situations. Nevertheless, they are
in general use and are helpful to our purpose. We will speak, first,
of educating the intelligent subject; second, of educating the cooperating democratic citizen; third, of educating the unconditional
follower within the political collective.

Although in England, the nation most faithful to old traditions,
the citizen is still legally called a subject, we generally connect
with this term the notion of the old absolutist governments which
regarded the inhabitants of their realms less as cooperating persons
than as servants. Subjects were bound to respect orders of the
prince issued under his name by his magistrates, most of whom
belonged to the nobility.

A considerable degree of authoritarianism can still be detected
in the famous dictum of Napoleon (who laid great value on being
regarded as the fulfiller rather than the executioner of the French
Revolution):

> Of all political questions, this one [on the importance of the teach-
> ing profession] deserves perhaps the most attention. There will be no
> political stability as long as there is no teaching body based on stable
> principles. So long as children are not taught whether they must be
> republicans or monarchists, Catholics or freethinkers, etc., the State
> will not constitute a nation but rest on vague and shifting foundations,
> ever exposed to disorder and change.[1]

---

1. From Napoleon I, *Mind, a Selection from His Written and Spoken Words*,
ed. and tr. by J. C. Herold, New York: Columbia Univ. Press, 1955, pp. 117 *ff*.
See also R. Ulich, *The Education of Nations, op. cit*, pp. 151 *ff*.

When we read any modern democratic constitution we sense immediately the difference between paternalism and the desire to produce a cooperating citizen. Authority no longer comes from above but from the people, who, through a system of checks and balances, try to prevent the usurpation of power by an entrenched or aggressive minority.

The spirit of democratic citizenship has been most forcefully expressed in the United States. We offer two examples of that expression.[2]

Thomas Jefferson wrote in a letter to James Madison, in 1787:

> Above all things, I hope that education of the common people will be attended to; convinced that on this good sense we may rely with the most security for the preservation of a due degree of liberty.

And George Washington said in 1790 in his First Message to Congress:

> Knowledge in every country is the surest basis of happiness. In one in which the measures of government receive their impressions so immediately from the sense of the community as in ours, it is proportionally essential.

Before and during the First World War one could reasonably hope that the spirit of statesmen like Jefferson and Washington would gradually spread over the civilized world. The army of the United States went to Europe to "make the world safe for democracy." And our historians when speaking of the political development of the Western world were generally satisfied with the distinction between democracy on the one hand, and despotic, or feudal, forms of government on the other. Democracy educated the younger generation for rational cooperativeness and had, therefore, the future on its side; despotism educated for obedience and was, therefore, obsolete. Later decades have complicated this simple antithesis by adding a third category, totalitarianism.

The physical and mental causes of this phenomenon are familiar enough, though their effect differs from country to country. They are: poverty, frustration, defeat, revenge, unemployment, lack of political education and experience, disgust at the quarrel of parties, demagoguery and class hatred, power complexes on the part of leaders, and—in some countries—the fear of the lower middle classes

---

2. For a wider selection see the chapter on "American Nationalism" in E. H. Wilds and K. V. Lottich, *The Foundations of Modern Education*, 3rd ed., New York: Holt, Rinehart and Winston, 1961, pp. 265 *ff.*

that they will "sink down into the proletariat." But behind and within the negative there have been at work essentially positive though diabolically misdirected rebellions against an emotionally barren and cruelly materialistic environment: the desire for devotion to something worthy of devotion, a sense of comradeship and heroism, and a desire for unity. Unless we are willing to see all these trends together we will never understand the complexity, the viciousness, but also the terrifying vigor of the human tragedy of totalitarianism. Totalitarianism was not merely a relapse into absolutism and the primitiveness of the herd instinct. Rather, it would have been impossible without a high level of ideological development, skillful planning, and cool sophistication on the part of leaders who knew how to combine the science of social engineering with the persuasive appeal of a new and better world.

There is, consequently, no common denominator for modern political collectivism. Although the following explanation is subject to criticism, it will perhaps clarify an understanding of our modern political and educational situation.

The difference between democratic and totalitarian countries lies in their different interpretations of the human person. Democratic countries may be called "free" because they permit the person to follow ethical criteria that transcend human institutions. Even the state stands under the judgment of those criteria.

To be sure, totalitarianism does not exclude improvement according to certain carefully prescribed routes, but it obstructs the way of the productive heretic. The voice and vision of the ever greater are eliminated. In a democratic society man is permitted to have an open mind and to engage in the fruitful competition of ideas, whereas in a totalitarian situation the collective spirit sets the limits. As we see in Soviet Russia and in communist China, the flowers of liberalism are not permitted to grow high.

Let us admit that openmindedness and the right of decent error may be endangered also in democracies, especially when they are in a state of tension. *The Open Mind* [3] is the title of a book by the American physicist J. Robert Oppenheimer, who has suffered for his diverging opinions concerning atomic policy. And we still remember the pressure exerted on schools and universities during the McCarthy era. However, Oppenheimer could

---

3. J. R. Oppenheimer, *The Open Mind*, New York: Simon and Schuster, 1955.

publish his lectures on this controversial topic and still remain Director of the Institute for Advanced Study at Princeton. Under Stalin a man of his quality would have been eliminated.

We have here arrived at one of the most difficult historical problems affecting the schools: How far can the privilege of freedom be extended without enabling the enemies of freedom to use it in order to destroy it? Whatever the philosophical meaning of freedom, every self-reliant society has insisted that its ideas about the right social order be supported by the schools. Therefore indoctrination is not only a totalitarian characteristic. Napoleon's statement about the relation between education and social stability is, after all, realistic. A vigorous nation wants to know that it can rely on its schools to transmit the values in which the people believe, whereas in a disrupted commonwealth the schools become inevitably involved in the battle of opinions. This was the case during and after the French Revolution and during the whole nineteenth century in France, and is to a degree even during the twentieth. With every change from monarchy inclined toward the Church, to democracy inclined toward liberalism, the government tried to change the schools.

Between the two World Wars the German Weimar Republic was unable to protect itself against its enemies in the government and in the schools. Having had little experience with the functional nature of liberty, it allowed first the old monarchists and then the nationalist-socialists to turn the minds of youth against democracy. The pragmatic Jefferson would not have permitted it. When he was afraid that the "slide into Toryism" might endanger the new republic, he refused to compromise on the appointment of a law professor at the University of Virginia. Thus, he wrote to James Madison in 1826: "In the selection of our Law Professor we must be rigorously attentive to his political principles." [4]

However, although even democracies cannot permit unlimited freedom, they differ from collectivist countries in the degree of indoctrination they demand. They preserve room for discussion and the spirit of tolerance, beginning on the elementary level and leading up to the intellectual delight of debate on the higher levels.

---

4. T. Jefferson, *The Writings,* ed. by A. A. Lipscomb, Washington, D.C., 1903–04, vol. 16, p. 156.

In contrast it has rightly been said that the whisper in schools, restaurants, and even within the family is the characteristic of totalitarianism. In Mussolini's Italy, but still more in Hitler's Germany and Stalin's Russia, pupils were rewarded for denouncing their teachers and even their parents. All children were gathered into membership in politically controlled youth organizations. Teachers were forced to discriminate between pupils from loyal families and pupils from suspect families, until, under the race-maniac Hitler and his henchmen, insanity reached its apex. But every collectivist system dislikes minorities.

One question has so far remained unanswered. Why has communism survived, while fascism and nazism, so we hope, are gone forever? During the first years following the Russian Revolution and again under Stalin, life in the Soviet Union was certainly no freer than life in Hitler's Germany. And why, in all likelihood, will Red China survive and, with its rapidly increasing population, become a greater and greater menace to its neighbors and the whole world?

There are several reasons: geographic location, natural resources, and the incredible patience of the population. But whether or not we like to admit it, the main reason for the survival of a communist state like the Soviet Union is that, in spite of many similarities, communism has never been the same as fascism or nazism. Communism is irrational in that it promotes the utopia of a classless workers' society throughout the world, but it is rational in its cool calculation of international advantages and its reliance on the power of science not only as a means of producing goods and arms but as a new form of faith and propaganda. As a consequence of this inherent rationality, communism is self-corrective to a degree. Probably none of its leaders believes today in the old Marxian slogans, though they are still used for political window-dressing. It was possible for Khrushchev to reveal to his nation the crimes of Stalin and—indirectly—of himself, whereas Mussolini and Hitler maneuvered themselves into a blind alley. Mussolini conjured the romantic image of the *Imperium Romanum,* and Hitler spoke of the Third Reich and the holiness of blood and soil. The Russians, on the other hand, believe in "materialistic dialectics."

This explains also the difference in the spirit and structure of the schools of these states. Neither in fascist Italy nor in nationalist-socialist Germany could a teacher have the feeling that he was working for progress. To be sure, modern tricks of motivation and of propaganda were skillfully applied to break young minds into the new pattern, but though the pattern was new it was also reactionary.

In contrast, the Soviet Republics have used their totalitarian power to change a nation with an 80 per cent rate of illiteracy into a nation with a school system that could be called Jeffersonian were it not a total contrast to Jefferson's spirit. After the first years of imitating Western progressivism and experimenting with Marx's ideas about labor schools, the Russians constructed a unilateral school system with a four-year elementary base, a six-year selective secondary school, and an enormous variety of post-secondary technical and scholarly institutions.

Certainly the system has proved to be effective. But we have already spoken about the broader criteria of human efficiency in the preceding chapter. Over a span of two thousand years the Greco-Roman-Christian tradition has created an ethical standard that is opposed to making the person a tool in the hands of a greater power, even that of the State. We may call it the struggle for human decency and the right to self-respect.

No one can decide today whether the Soviet Union will be able to instill these values (without which there can be no real citizenship) into its internal and international politics. As we know from an analysis of revolutions and violent ideologies, the fire of chauvinism burns out slowly. Until it does, the noncommunist nations will have no excuse for lowering their vigilance.

Suggestions for Class Discussion and Further Investigation

1. In what ways does the form of government influence the kind of education that will develop within a nation?
2. When a democratic nation is taken over by a totalitarian government, what changes are likely to occur in the educational system?
3. Compare the kinds of schools that have developed under fascism with those that have developed under communism. Pay particular attention to the differential development of elementary, secondary, and higher education under each form of government.
4. Contrast indoctrination with education. Can you identify

any examples of indoctrination in American education today?
Is indoctrination an inevitable part of education?

5. Are there any legitimate limits to academic freedom? How far can the privilege of freedom be extended without incurring the risk that the enemies of freedom will use it to destroy freedom?

6. When you examine the schools of various nations—and then recall the fate of those nations—do you conclude that universal education leads necessarily to progress or to national survival?

Chapter Ten

Education for the Future

Chapters Eight and Nine provided no support for the general belief that education leads necessarily to progress. True, the amount of information distributed by our schools is immensely larger than in earlier times. But information is not the same as formation. Never before have the states of the world paid so much attention to education within and outside their boundaries. Even the enormous sums of money they spend are not commensurate with the magnitude of the new tasks and demands that have arisen. But have we more "truth" in Pestalozzi's sense, or more "culture" in Emerson's sense? Recently Jean Guéhenno, a member of the Académie Française, wrote an article in *Figaro* in which he welcomed the plan of his government to build twenty *"maisons de culture,"* or cultural centers, throughout the country. However, he felt compelled to offer the authorities a reminder:

> Culture is not a parade, nor is it a fair, a great spectacle, or a circus. It certainly is something more intimate and private. It is a concern of the soul, a delight, a joy and a debate with oneself that prepares us for ever more delicate and profound communications with other persons.[1]

Despite the world's yearning for peace the cold war continues, and parents anxiously ask themselves what the future will bring to their children. Communism and its forms of education and propaganda have made political and cultural satellites of nations that had hoped that the sacrifices of the Second World War would give them the freedom of self-decision. Looking back at education as it has been during the past decades and as it is still today in many places, one discovers a frantic emphasis on science, but at the same time a frightening lack of truly human purpose. Apparently education has alienated itself from the perennial concerns of mankind. Especially in the United States, it has lost contact with the

---

1. J. Guéhenno, "Circulation de la pensée," *Figaro*, January 29, 1963.

philosophia perennis, partly because modern philosophy itself has lost that contact.

The advantages of schooling have been extended to members of the population who at the beginning of this century would not have dreamed of sending their sons and daughters to a secondary school, much less a college or a university. And for this extension of opportunity we cannot be sufficiently grateful. But length and quantity of education are not enough, nor is mere intellectual skill. Unless knowledge leads men to ever-deeper commitments, however simply understood and performed, the loss is greater than the gain.

The literature of all Western nations reflects a pessimistic mood. It smiles at the older idealism; it reveals neither the realism of an Émile Zola with all its deep sympathies for the sufferings and errors of mankind, nor the heretical humor of an Anatole France. It is, to use the term loosely, often "existentialist" with a negativistic flavor and just as often preoccupied with sex. Many of our adolescents receive from that literature their images of life.

But there is also reason for hope. First of all, every nation has been seriously concerned with improving the structure of education. Although, save Russia, none has had the courage to reconstruct its secondary school system as thoroughly as England did after passing the Education Act of 1944, they have all worked toward a more equitable distribution of the privilege of advanced learning than existed before the First World War. Whereas the United States has lost its former attitude of complacency, based on the democratic organization of its school system, it has now realized —partly as a result of the Sputnik—that mass production, even on higher levels of schooling, is no substitute for high standards. The old unilateral or "single ladder" system has given way to an immense variety of patterns, all designed to stimulate individual talent. Thus the European and the American systems are approaching each other in both aim and structure, although the old countries still see the best guarantee of high achievement as an early separation of the gifted pupils (ages ten to twelve) from the average.

Furthermore, new developments in psychology promise to influence our schools. The European countries are coming to understand the wide uses of experimental psychology and psychometrics that they have so far neglected. And American psychology is beginning to extricate itself from the grip of behaviorism which, following the *tabula rasa* theory of John Locke, considered human learning primarily in terms of a stimulus-response mechanism and carefully avoided any concept that might remind the student of the active and uniting center in man, variously called mind, self, personality, or even soul. Not without good reason did Joseph Wood Krutch in his book, *The Measure of Man* [2] point to the affinity between behaviorism and collectivism. For neither has any regard for those transcendent values of the human person which we connect with the idea of freedom of the will.[3]

Of course, neither will the new psychology lift the veil of mystery from the phenomenon of the human person. Unless scholarship advances far beyond the present stage, the answers to the question "What is man?" will have to be left to metaphysics and religious and poetic intuitions. While some theories may lead us farther away from the truth, others may lead us closer to it and at the same time help us to correct the fallacies and superstitions of older mythical conceptions.

On the other hand, the more psychology passes beyond the descriptive toward the existential stage of investigation, the more it will itself be confronted with questions that have so far been relegated to intuitional methods of search. For the problem will arise as to which deep forces in the person make learning, education, and communication possible. For the Greeks and John the Apostle it was the *logos,* or the all-permeating and all-ordering spiritual principle in the universe; for the mystics, it was the divine *pneuma;* for others, God; for still others, nature or the creation; for Kant, the transcendental apperception; for the romantic idealists and Emerson, the "World Spirit." All these answers may be rejected by the positivist and the agnostic, but both will have to acknowledge that the problem exists and they will thus help us to gain a greater clarity about where evidence ends and guessing begins.

Furthermore, we will have to recognize the defectiveness of all

---

2. J. W. Krutch, *The Measure of Man,* Indianapolis: Bobbs-Merrill, 1954.
3. In this connection see: G. W. Allport, *Becoming: Basic Considerations for a Psychology of Personality,* New Haven: Yale Univ. Press, 1955; J. S. Bruner, *The Process of Education,* Cambridge, Mass.: Harvard Univ. Press, 1960; and P. A. Bertocci and R. M. Millard, eds., *Personality and the Good: Psychological and Ethical Perspectives,* New York: David McKay, 1963. This latter contains an analysis of the works of Adler, Allport, Freud, Fromm, Horney, Jung, and Maslow in their relation to the ethical problem.

endeavors to isolate education from ethics. If education fails to understand itself as a part of culture with its endless striving for better and more universal achievements, it will degenerate into a mere social technique that can be used for evil as well as for good. Often it has been nothing but that.

The attempt of the new psychology of personality to understand the human being in the wholeness of his relations to himself, his fellow men, and the universe will also lead to a better understanding between education and the religious tradition. Historically speaking, up to the eighteenth century and in many countries even today the schools and the churches were closely connected. Often, however, it was a most unhappy alliance. The tensions between the so-called secular and the denominational concepts of education will persist, for they are intimately associated with the conflicts of *Weltanschauung* that permeate our civilization, Western and non-Western. But on the basis of a new "philosophical anthropology" (toward which modern psychology is leading and which actually will be a revival of century-old endeavors to arrive at a *logia* of man), the secularists may discover that a religious outlook toward life is not necessarily identical with an established creed that is eager to strangle the freedom of teaching. They might acknowledge that one cannot call a person educated who is ignorant of the impact of religious thought on the minds of poets, artists, philosophers, and even scientists. Thus, the secularists will present to advocates of denominational instruction in public schools a much more serious challenge than they did at the time of dogmatic hostility toward anything that reminded them even vaguely of ecclesiastical influences. Movements of thought that attempted to develop an authentic religious view of life without any connection with, sometimes even in opposition to, established churches appear today in many countries. These movements indicate that we live in an era of transformation of man's spiritual consciousness. The old polarity of formal piety and atheism has become obsolete.

Besides the widening of educational horizons through new developments in psychology, philosophy, and religion, a momentous historical force has appeared in the form of our awareness of the global interdependence of mankind. This cannot fail to have a profound impact on our schools. They will have to teach their students that one cannot become a good citizen without some knowledge of the lives of other nations.

This must not mean that our schools should burden the minds of the young with incoherent pieces of information about the seven continents, although our typical instruction in history and geography is utterly inadequate. Our teachers will have to find a way of rooting the young in their own tradition (for uprooted people have just as much difficulty understanding mankind as do those who are afraid of looking beyond their own garden fence). But at the same time they will have to awaken in their pupils a sense of responsibility for the unity of all members of the human race irrespective of color, creed, and nationality. The old questions will have to be raised: Am I my brother's keeper? Who is my neighbor? Is he the man across the street or a suffering human being in a far-away country?

As has become increasingly clear, we cannot even separate our future from that of a Russian communist. From a merely selfish point of view, his decisions may be more crucial to us than those of people in our immediate environment. We should, therefore, know about him. But fear—though undeniably a factor in politics —would be a base motive for an international ethics of man. What we need today is a combination of realistic knowledge of how things stand and a confidence in man's ability to form them as they should be.

Never have the demands on education been so immense as they are today. The old foundations of Western civilization are being shaken by new and conflicting philosophies and, still more, by spiritual indifference. Incisive changes have occurred in the role of the family, the role of women, and in our whole social and economic structure. Our scientific knowledge and its application to space and the problems of peace and war make our lives very different from those of earlier generations. But at the very time when we fear that our own education is faced with unconquerable tasks, a host of newly emerging nations asks us to export it to their own population. Severe mistakes have been made on both sides; but we begin to learn from them. International organizations, among them UNESCO, will cooperate with the individual nations and their schools. Our universities and their departments of education are beginning slowly—alas, very slowly—to commit themselves to the training of an adequate international teaching staff. Yet no one can foresee the final effect of all these enterprises.

No doubt they will destroy old and indigenous cultures whose leaders are torn by the conflict between the old and the new. The frightening question is whether those leaders really know what they want and what they ought to want. Do they merely want more machines, more industry, and through these more employment, food, housing, and arms? Or do they want also what we might call "a good life" in its total sense, comprising both body and soul?

The history of education joins with all history: When it looks into the future, it ends with a question mark.

Suggestions for Class Discussion and Further Investigation

1. What would be the long-range effect of an educational system that attempted to be ethically neutral—that is, one that provided factually accurate information but avoided all value judgments? Has such education ever been attempted? Can education remain completely neutral? Can there be complete ethical neutrality in interpersonal relations?

2. Select an "emerging nation" of which you have some knowledge and trace the development of its educational system from precolonial times through its colonial period and into nationalism. What kinds of crises have been faced? What have been the solutions?

3. How has the cold war affected education in the United States? In the Soviet Union? What has been the effect on liberal education and on technical and scientific education?

4. How does our growing awareness of the global interdependence of mankind affect education throughout the world?

5. Would it be possible to design a culturally neutral educational program—i.e., one that had no cultural bias? If such an attempt were made, what language should be used for instruction?

Index

134

Index

Index

Kandel, I. L., 105
Kant, Immanuel, 72, 89, 94, 97, 98, 129
Khrushchev, Nikita, 124
Kierkegaard, Sören Aabye, 77
Kindergarten, 82, 115
Knighthood, 50
Krutch, Joseph Wood, 129

La Chalotais, Louis René de Caradeuc de, 91
La Mettrie, Julien Offray de, 88
Languet, Hubert, 75
Law, 32–33
Leibniz, Gottfried Wilhelm von, 98
Leo III, Pope, 32
Leo XIII, Pope, 110
Lessing, Gotthold Ephraim, 54, 89
Licei, 114
Light, 66, 87
Locke, John, 15, 75, 88, 92, 129
Logan, James, 29
Logos, 12, 21, 67, 129
Louis XI, 7, 58
Louis XIV, 73
Luther, Martin, 54, 55, 61, 66
Lycées, 114
Lycurgus, 23

Madison, James, 121, 123
Maimonides, Moses, 47
Marcel, Gabriel, 77
Marcus Aurelius, 40
Maria Theresa, 93
Marius, Gaius, 30
Marx, Karl, 6, 15, 88, 106, 108, 124
Mathematics, 12, 25, 26, 45, 87, 97
Mather, Cotton, 69
McCarthy, Joseph, 122
Medici, Lorenzo de, 56, 101
Medici family, 60
Medicine, 26
Menander, 25
"Method," 65–66
Michelangelo, 55, 56
Middle Ages, 4, 6, 15, 21, 42–52, 53, 92
Milton, John, 49
Mohammed, 43
Montaigne, Michel de, 92
More, Sir Thomas, 55
Moses, 33, 34, 40
Muslims, 54
Mussolini, Benito, 124

Napoleon Bonaparte, 120, 123
Nation, and education, 7–8
National Herbartian Society, 98
Nature, 64, 66, 68, 71, 72, 73, 74, 77, 79, 80, 83
Nazism, 124
New Education fellowship, 106

Newton, Sir Isaac, 65, 67
Nicaea, council, 42
Nietzsche, Friedrich, 109

Odoacer, 42
Oppenheimer, J. Robert, 122
Order, Roman education for, 28–33
Organic development (circles of experience), 73, 76, 77, 83, 96
Origen, 26, 39, 40, 46
Oxford University, 6, 101

Pansophia, 64, 70
Pax Romana, 32
Pericles, 24
Pestalozzi, Johann Heinrich, 73, 74, 75–79, 80, 81, 83, 96, 98, 106, 127
Peter the Great, 93
Petrarch, Francesco, 53, 54, 56, 60
"Philanthropinism," 15, 84
Philip II, 22
Philo of Alexandria, 35
Picasso, Pablo, 64
Pico della Mirandola, Giovanni, 56
Pius II, Pope, 59
Pius XI, Pope, 109
Plato, 19, 20, 21, 22, 24, 25, 26, 30, 36, 49, 101, 104, 119
Pluralistic society, American concept of, 100–07
Plutarch, 26, 27, 28
Poggio Bracciolini, Giovanni Francesco, 45, 55
Pole, Reginald, 60
Popes, 43
Portugal, 91
Pragmatism, 113
"Presentations," 95
Princeton University, 123
Program of studies, 13–17
Progressive education, 97, 103, 104–07
Protagoras, 20, 22
Protestantism, 56, 63, 89
Psychology, 112, 113, 128
Psychometry, 112, 113, 128
Public Schools, English, 15, 111, 114
Pythagoras, 25

Quadrivium, 21, 45, 47
Quakers, 69
Quintilian, Marcus Fabius, 31, 45, 55, 59

Rabelais, François, 92
Rationalism, 86–99, 100–03
Reason, the Age of, 86–99; and education, 12–13; Greek education for, 18–28
Ratke, Wolfgang, 68
Red China; see Communist China
Reformation, 9, 56, 58, 63
Renaissance, 14, 15, 53–61